An English Town
Market Rasen

The Fabulous Fifties - Myself, Trevour Bakin, Brian Bennett

Picture left: Hannalore and brother John outside No. 2 Willingham Road. Above the front door states - 1888. The Halpenny Family Home that should have stayed a home. Picture Right: At Crane Bridge with ice cream from Mason's Tuck Shop. Left to right: John Sutton, Myself, Dick White & Dick Fieldsend.
Out of the 16 Sweet Shops in the 1950's, only Garnets made it into the 21st Century.

5 pubs – The Gordon Arms, the King's Head, the George, the Aston Arms and the Red Lion, that have survived into the 21st Century. It was the pubs that helped to make the town … cheers!

An English Town
Market Rasen

by

Bruce Barrymore Halpenny

In our back garden at 2 Willingham Road. My father, Uncle George and myself. It is 1945 and Uncle George has just returned from Italy ... You can read about him in my book, ***"Bullets in the Morning ... Bullets at Night – The Italian Campaign"***
ISBN 0-9547774-1-7

ANZIO

First edition – first published 25 May 2004

Halpenny, Bruce Barrymore
AN ENGLISH TOWN – MARKET RASEN
1. English Market Town - Halpenny Family, Market Rasen racecourse,
2. Market Rasen - Lincolnshire
I. Title
ISBN : 0-9547774-0-9

Published by ANZIO
483 Green Lanes
LONDON
N13 4BS
England

Internet : www.anzio.co.uk
E-mail : admin@anzio.co.uk

NOTICE: ANZIO *does not accept unsolicited manuscripts*

CONTENTS

ACKNOWLEDGEMENTS

The search for information has been painstaking over a number of years, and many people have been eager to help, but a few Rasen people could not be bothered and that sums up the changing times. I have interviewed hundreds of people, and very fortunate to get the facts – much I could remember – from my mother, Eleanor May, who had a crystal sharp memory. I acknowledge, with gratitude, my old school friend Brian Ayre with help in sorting material, photographs and interviewing people. Among the many – sadly many not here now but did help and still get a mention – Frank and Tilly Burks; Jim Batchelor; Bill Blanchard; G.W.Capes; Dr. Michael Eames; Dick Fieldsend; Frank Fieldsend; Mrs Fisher; Bryan Forway; Henny Goddard, Deputy Editor of 'Real Countryside' Countryside Alliance; John Halpenny; Mrs Elizabeth Hardy; George Hubbert; Taffy James; Jack Maltby; Derek Marwood; Tom Pickering; Martin Pickering; Harold Plumtree; Racing Post Editorial-Dean Willard; Terry Senior; Philip Sharp; Teddy Sharp; Henry Sheehan; Fred Sorfleet; Mrs Staves; Bud Stevenson (Canada)

Bruce Barrymore Halpenny
Italy

Above left, Bruce Barrymore Halpenny with Dennis McCarthy on BBC Radio Nottingham, and above right, Bruce Barrymore Halpenny (in the chair) with Keith Skues on Radio Hallam – Sheffield in 1980's. Keith cut his teeth (and fingers getting on the ship in a gale!) at Radio Caroline

GLOSSARY

Acre - 40 perches in length, and four in breadth. (10 square chains)
Amice - a Liturgical vesmment consisting of an oblong piece of cloth usually of white linen, worn about the neck and shoulders and partly under the alb.
Berewicks - are manors within manors.
BOAT – Byway Open to All Traffic.
Bordars - cottagers with a small piece of land.
Bovate - a bovate is as much as one ox can plough in a year, this was about 15 acres.
A Carucate, Carve, or Plough Land - generally 120 acres or eight oxgangs.
Cordwainer – a worker in Cordovan leather or cordwain; a shoemaker.
Domesday Book – survey of England made by William the Conqueror in 1085-87. It was printed in two volumes in 1783-93 and 1816.
Geld - means of payment, tax.
Glebe – land the income from which forms part of the revenue of a church benefice.
Heriot - a fine due to the lord of the manor.
Hide - an uncertain quantity, generally about 120 acres.
Horn Book - a child's primer, so called because formerly covered by a sheet of transparent horn to protect it, and having on it the alphabet and other rudiments such as the digits and often the Lord's Prayer.
Husbandman – a working farmer.
Infangtheof - the power of passing judgement on theft.
A Knight's fee - five hides.
Mercer – one who deals in silk, linen and woollen wares.
Messuage – a dwelling house with its outbuildings and adjoining lands.
Merchet or Maiden Rent - was a payment to the lord of the manor, in commutation of his right with the virgin bride on the marriage of a vassal's daughter.
Oxgang - means the going of an ox and implies the same amount of land as a bovate.
Pagan – heathen; an idolater.
Papist – a Roman Catholic.

Perch – linear measure. 1 Perch = 5 ½ yards. Square Perch = 30 ¼ square yards
Pix - (or Pyx) a box, tabernacle, or a container used ecclesiastically to hold the reserved sacrament on the altar of Holy Table.
Quit-Rent - is a rent reserved in grants of land, by the payment of which the tenant is quit from all other service.
Quoits - a game played with a flat and heavy ring for throwing at a pin, at about 20 yards distance.
A Rood – 40 perches – the forth part of an acre.
See - a seat or centre of the power or authority of a bishop or archbishop; the authority of the pope or court of Rome.
Socage – a feudal tenure by service other than knight service.
Soke – a district or liberty.
Socmen - were tenants holding land under a so cage tenure.
Sokeman - a man who is under the soke of another, a tenant by socage.
Soken - a district held by socage; the privilege of taking toll for grinding grain in a certain district.
Theam - was a manorial jurisdiction.
Turnpike road - A road on which turnpikes or tollgates are established by law.
Vassal - a tenant holding lands under a lord.
Villane – a serf attached to a farm.
Virgate, or Yard Land – an old English measure of land - 40 acres.
Viz – namely

INTRODUCTION

Market Rasen goes back to the time of the Romans who did much to cultivate the land that we take for granted today. Chapter 2 sets out to explain the name of the town and the many ways of spelling it, which occurred through the ages. In the Domesday Book it was just referred to as Rase. Where I have quoted from old records and letters I have retained the spelling of the period, so that the reader can see the many ways the town of Market Rasen was spelt, and how words have become modernized through the ages.

Market Rasen was the launch pad for the Tennyson family, who climbed to the very top of the social ladder, and despite that very fact, for some reason, the Tennyson family shunned the little market town, that had helped take them to the top.

From the open fields came the enclosures in 1779, and Market Rasen began to grow, and many famous people … which could have included many famous Romans who may have already done so in the past … were to visit the town, one being Charles Dickens, whose career as a writer of fiction began in 1833 with short stories and essays in periodicals, and in 1837 his comic novel *The Pickwick Papers*, made him the most popular author of his time in England. He stayed at Market Rasen and was quoted as saying, *"It was the most sleepiest town in England."* Coming from Dickens, who made it to the top of the literary world with *'Christmas Carol'* and the like, it could well have been meant as a compliment. After a tankard or two of Mrs Smith's fine ale, it could well have been *'the most sleepiest town in England.'* I think it was meant as a compliment. He never said it was the most backward, or the dirtiest, or the most ignorant town in England, and he would have done … had it been so.

In one way or another, Market Rasen has always had a connection or interest in the wars of the world. In October 1857, Market Rasen had a day of fasting for the Indian Mutiny, and all denominations held separate services. But the greatest link for the town must be the fact that the horse the Duke of Wellington rode at the Battle of Waterloo was bred at Market Rasen. How nice to have seen a statue of the Duke of Wellington and his horse Copenhagen in the market place.

During the Second World War, Market Rasen was surrounded by bomber airfields and for many young aircrews, Rasen was their last place on earth, for many failed to return from bombing sorties. How nice to have seen a bomber on a plinth in memory to those who failed to return, and for the new generation to see the part played by Market Rasen during the dark years of war. It could have been sited on the Willingham Road between the De Aston Grammar School and the racecourse, with a parking area, or on the site of the old white house opposite the racecourse on the Willingham Road. Market Rasen council and higher council big wigs, let pass this golden opportunity - as usual.

In 1885 it was stated that the population of Lincolnshire was purely English, except so far as it was mixed with Danish blood [which I explain in a moment].

Ignoring the darker years beginning in the late 1800's, Market Rasen had remarkable prosperity. You only have to see the 1872 list of Market Rasen traders in chapter 11, to see what a hive of activity the town had become.

With the march of time, and the waywardness of the council at all levels, Market Rasen stopped making gas, the station roof was removed and taken back to London, the town ceased to have a cinema and a main street Post Office, and dozens of little shops closed, and with them service and civility and many trades and skills.

For market towns such as Market Rasen, people had to make their own amusement, and the Trading Fair was the pleasure fair, which replaced the old horse fair. Going to the seaside was a special occasion right up until the late 1950's.

Market Rasen was born and brought up on religion, and I can remember the enjoyable times at Sunday school. Every day in the junior school we had to sing the prayer for lunch before going to eat, *"Be Present At Our Table Lord."* It was a great pleasure to sing it and I have never regretted it. At the De Aston Grammar School there was Assembly every morning, and I looked forward to it and singing hymns. The one I remember most (and liked) is, *"For Those In Peril On The Sea."* For that, one could [and I did] sing with gusto. Sadly, the De Aston Grammar School is now a Comprehensive School and the teachers have lost respect. Good manners cost nothing. Masters in my day had the respect of both pupils and parents.

Even in a small district such as Market Rasen, it can be said that nothing so much begets change as change of a generation. Since the First World War the new generation growing up is no longer approaching local life with the same targets or the same point of view as those who have gone before. Today, the names are different; the whole background of values and priorities tends all the time to be on the move.

Since the 1950's the real Colossus has been the continual rising of public expenditure, on the schools and houses as well as in other related fields, and it has dominated the rural scene to an extent not previously envisaged. In the 21st century it is the mighty conglomerates that rule and dictate world policy.

We got rid of the pagan gods from England way back in the year 600 after Augustine, a Roman monk, came to preach the Christian faith. The church and religion no longer play, due to the filthy Godless acts of those in charge of young children, the relative part in town affairs. It would be nice to turn back the clock and listen to the choir singing, and the church bells peeling out in happiness after another joyous harvest. The Wesleyans and Methodists [for a change united] in full song. Alleluia. The Sunday school parties the like of which are now forgotten.

My grandfather was Charles Hall chimney sweep and shopkeeper before the turn of the last century. They had the greengrocer shop at 54 Queen Street, Market Rasen, and after the First World War, Harvey Halpenny went back to Canada to be demobilised and then returned to Market Rasen, having married Eleanor May Hall, and they purchased No.2 Willingham Road, which became the Halpenny Family home. I was the youngest of a Family of five, Joan, Derek, Gordon, John, and myself, Bruce Barrymore Halpenny. Sadly, Harvey Halpenny died in January 1972 at the age of 80 and his wife Eleanor May, passed away seven years later on January 1, 1979, and was laid to rest in the cemetery at Market Rasen.

The Nettleship family were a main force in the town, but more for their ends, not the town. Their manor house, built in the 1920's on the site of three cottages, has since been pulled down and a new manor built nearby. The lawns and orchard of the old manor house have sprouted little boxes called bungalows, no thought given to the fact that one can only have bad luck if a property is built on an old orchard.

Market Rasen, untouched by razzamatazz, always had an uphill struggle because of the waywardness of the council at all levels. The council, in its mindless wisdom, did nothing to preserve the White Hart Hotel that made Rasen a town.

Today there is more greed and selfishness than we used to know years ago. Also, vandalism, violence and drugs are a big problem today. The 1980's showed a move from the large towns towards the smaller towns. I do know, that Market Rasen could be the best, for it has a lot to offer, but it needs people with vision who want to help Market Rasen; people like Mrs Smith, Mrs Eleanor May Halpenny and Victor Lucas. When I last saw Luke, it was on a Good Friday. He was not well, and we went to see him for he wanted to see our newborn son – Baron, before we returned to Italy. When we arrived at his race-course home, he was in bed; and, against my wishes, Eileen got him up … and I'm pleased she did, for it did him a power of good, for his eyes sparkled as he held Baron on his knees. We talked over old times and he still laughed about the race day sale; and the time he fell down in the isle in the cinema in Lincoln, with his leg bolt upright … but that is another story. Sadly, those people have gone, and the politically correct pea brains in charge do not have that vision or interest for the town.

Bruce Barrymore Halpenny.
Italy.

Post scriptum: I would very much like to hear from the young Signorina who is looking at the person taking the photograph shown at the end of Chapter 24 –The 1950's. Contact me via the publishers.

Myself and my good friend Brian Ayre

CHAPTER 1

THE ROMANS

Centurion

The name of Lincolnshire is derived from its chief town. The Saxon name was Lindocollyne, which was derived from Lindum or Lindecollina., the Roman name of its capital, and has been, by subsequent and gradual alterations, remodelled into its present form. Under the reign of the Norman conquerors, Lincolnshire was designated by the name of Nicolshire, but this could have come about owing to the imperfect pronunciation of the Normans, and Incol. or Lincol, could have been misread as Nicol.

The ancient inhabitants of Lincolnshire were the Coritani and at the time of the Roman invasions in the year 54 BC; was very sparsely populated.

The dwellings of the ancient Britons were scattered about and generally situated on the bank of some rivulet, or on the skirt of some wood or forest, for the convenience of hunting, and pasture for their cattle. Caesar describes the towns of the Britons, as *"tracts of woody country surrounded by a mound or ditch, for the security of themselves and their cattle, against incursions of their enemies."*

The ancient Britain's were clothed in the skins of the animals, which disputed with them the dominion or the country. Caesar first planted the standard of civilization in Britain and by the year 47, a frontier had been established from Exeter to the Humber.

In the first 20 years of occupation, some progress had been made in spreading Roman civilisation. The natives began to erect towns and cities, and to adopt the habits, customs and manners of their conquerors. Their agricultural knowledge was increased by the Romans, and they cultivated the soil with assiduity. The face of the country very soon exhibited a new appearance. The art of brick making was introduced and soon houses and walls grew up all through the occupied territory. Towns and cities were founded, and productive meadows and cornfields. The Romans also built forts and stations. The military walls that were built prove to us just how clever the Romans were in military skill, for the positions chosen for these defence works were perfect, when we consider the conditions of the times and the requirements.

The Romans commenced the drainage of the marshes and fens of Lincolnshire, and one of the greatest works is the Cardyke, which extends from the River Welland, on the southern side of the county, to the River Witham, near Fiskerton, to within a few miles of Lincoln. Its channel, for nearly the whole of this course, an extent of about 40 miles, is 60 feet in width.

By cutting the Cardyke, the Romans prevented the waters from deluging the county, for this great canal receives from the hills, all the drainage and flowing waters which take an easterly course, and which, but for this 'catch water' drain, would serve to inundate the Fens. The Fossdyke, another canal attributed to the Romans, extends from the Witham at Lincoln, to the Trent, near Torksey.

During the Roman government in Britain, Lincolnshire was included within the province of Flavia Caesariensis, and had a number of military stations established in various parts of it. The Romans also established many forts and stations of inferior rank, in various parts of the county, one being at Linwood, near Market Rasen.

Another close to Market Rasen was at Ludford, which was undoubtedly a Roman station at the head or the River Bane. Many coins and other Roman remains have at different times been dug up, which bears out its Roman role.

The Romans built Rasen as a main rest area for their cavalry, for within easy reach of the Frontline Stations and Lincoln. The Romans taught the ancient Brits tanning. The skins of the mammalia consist of two principal layers, of which the inner is called the *corium* [Latin] or 'true skin', which is what is used. It is an art, which the Romans had perfected [see my bespoke Italian coccodrillo shoes]. The bark of the oak is one of the oldest and perhaps the most satisfactory of tanning materials; but by the 1800's its place was taken by other vegetable products.

At the time of the Romans, there was a plentiful supply of both oak trees and water. So a perfect site for the station by the River

Rase, its role being to feed and rest the horses and men of the Roman cavalry. Therefore, there had to be drinking houses; indeed, there were many thatched inns at Rasen, long before the days of the Greyhound, hence did not survive. The site was perfect for horses, and history has proved this to be so.

The role of the Ludford and Caistor stations would be 'lookout' duties for raiders from the Humber and the east, and at the first sign of trouble, would get word back to Rasen.

It would be nice to think that Rasen was an early Roman tourist resort … Why not? It is a fact that thatched hovels were soon replaced by good dwelling houses during the Roman occupation, and the tastes and conditions of the people were improved in many directions. Baths were introduced, and cleanly habits became general, the practice of smearing the body all over with mud and coloured earth disappeared, and it became the fashion to adopt Roman manners and customs. The dress of the well-to-do classes became quite splendid, and during the 3rd century, it would have puzzled a stranger to distinguish a Briton of the upper class from Roman.

It became during this period a fashion for the wealthy Romans to come to this country – it was part of the Roman Empire - for the summer months, much in the same way as English go today to the shores of the Mediterranean to escape an English winter. Those wealthy visitors built villas in favourable positions, and occasionally the remains of these holiday resorts are discovered in different parts of the country. Just after the First World War the foundations of one were unearthed in Greenwich Park, on the top of a hill, which commands a splendid view of the Thames and the county of Essex.

Just after the Second World War, one was discovered not far from Market Rasen. The floor of the villa, made of small bits of mosaic embedded in cement, could be seen in perfect condition. I was out on my cycle with my air pistol when I came across these two men digging. They saw me and I went to them. It turned out they were not digging, but filling the Roman villa floor. I was told never to tell anyone, and I gave my word not to do so. I have kept my word and will continue to keep the precise location a secret for fear of vandals and looters. It is a fact it was not a military building, it looked to have been a large villa, and it is in a splendid position. The

Roman owners could well have visited Market Rasen, thus making Rasen an early, if not the first, tourist resort.

As stated, I will not reveal the location of the Roman Villa, but I will just say, that as a young lad, I found a lot of Roman pottery at Linwood Warren – opposite the entrance to the golf course – that was near to Grammy Robbins gang hut. All found in sand, only a foot or so down … Good hunting. You might be lucky and find a pot of Roman coins. It is a fact that Romans were there, and there were no safes in those days.

The Roman road system was an outstanding transportation network of the ancient world, extending from Britain to the Tigris-Euphrates and, from the Danube to Spain and North Africa. The Romans built 50,000 miles of hard-surfaced highway, primarily for military purposes. The Romans only selected routes that had springs or rivers at even sections so that the Roman Legions always had water en-route. For the benefit of the reader, a Roman Legion comprised 3,000-foot soldiers; this was later increased to 6,000-foot soldiers with a compliment of cavalry; so water was very important. No country can possibly develop without roads, and the better they are, the more rapidly will other improvements follow. The road is a great civilizing agent, bringing together the towns and cities of a country. Good roads encourage travelling and increase trade.

The three great Roman roads which passed through Lincolnshire were the Ermine street, extending from London (Bishopsgate), via Stamford, Colsterworth, Navenby, Boothby Graffo, Lincoln, and thence to York, crossing the Humber at Brough; the Fossway, which traversed Britain from south-west to north-east, ran from the coast near Saltfleetby to Lincoln, and thence to Bath; and the Saltway, which extended from the salt mines at Droitwich to the coast near Wainfleet, passing near Grantham, Sleaford, and Tattershall, which was a Roman station (Drurobrivis). Market Rasen was in reach of the Roman roads and there are traces of one from Burgh to Caistor.

The Roman language did not take hold on the Britons, as it did on the Gauls and the inhabitants of Spain. The Romans were good colonists. They were wise, very wise. Some have thought that we also owe a debt of gratitude to the Romans for destroying the ancient Druid religion, which they found supreme in Britain when they came. It was contrary to their usual practice to interfere with the religions of the races they conquered, but in the case of the Druids they displayed great wisdom. These Druids were a body who practically ruled in all religious matters, and looked after the public and private sacrifices. They settled all disputes amongst the people, bestowing all rewards and punishments, and anyone who refused to abide by their awards was shut out from all the great sacrificial ceremonies, a punishment dreaded by all people. As all the men of the tribes had to render military service whenever occasion arose, and the Druids only were excused, there were a good many of the less warlike youths who found refuge from the army by becoming priests.

The Romans saw that it was impossible to allow a religion to exist which interfered with the civil duties of the people, and which purposely kept them in ignorance, so they made short work of the Druids and destroyed their power forever.

The downfall of the tyranny of the Druids prepared the way for the introduction of Christianity, which took place during the latter part of the Roman occupation.

In the early part of the 5th century, the Romans found it necessary to withdraw their troops from Britain to assist in defending Italy against barbarian invaders; and, in 448, the Romans finally relinquished all possession, power and authority in Britain.

After the Romans had gone, the banks, drains and sluices, which they had formed, were neglected, and a great part of the county that they had brought into cultivation soon returned to its original fenny state. The country sank into a state of anarchy. During the Anglo-Saxon era, Lincolnshire was incorporated within the kingdom of Mercia; and, during the establishment of these petty kingdoms, the Saxons were in constant warfare with the Romanized Britons; and after these were subdued, they were repeatedly embroiled in conflicts with each other. I mention the Saxons at this period, for the mythology of the Saxons is interwoven with the English language. From objects of their worship, the names of our days have been derived. The first and second days in the week they dedicated to the Sun and the Moon; hence - Sunday and Monday; the third and fourth were dedicated to Tuisco and Woden; hence - Tuesday and Wednesday; the fifth, sixth and seventh, in like manner, to Thor, Frea and Seator; hence – Thursday, Friday and Saturday.

In the year 870 the Danes landed at Humberston in Lincolnshire, and they raped and plundered the county; at which time, the famous and ancient monastery at Bardney was destroyed, the monks being all massacred in the church without mercy.

The Danes had passed through Market Rasen, plundered what they could and the local wenches paid the price with the Danes; hence the reference that the population of old Lincolnshire mixed with Danish blood.

Count Algor and two knights, Wilbert and Leofric, joined Osgot, the Sheriff of Lincoln, with the Lincolnshire forces, which totalled some five hundred men, and they defeated the Danes on St. Maurice's day.

Soon after the Norman Conquest Lincoln became one of the most popular populous cities in England, full of trade, and resorted to both by land and water. Because of its close proximity to Lincoln and on a main road, Market Rasen must have benefited from the trade at Lincoln, which was a main and important Roman town during the period it was part of the Roman Empire. So we see that the Romans did much for this little island. They were a great people, and the whole world owes much to their wisdom, learning, and experience.

CHAPTER 2

A TOWN IS BORN

The county of Lincoln is divided into three parts or provinces, viz, Holland, Kesteven and Lindsey. These divisions are subdivided into twenty-seven hundreds, and five sokes. These hundreds and wapentakes contain 630 parishes; one city, Lincoln; and 32 market towns, one being Market Rasen, which is pleasantly seated on the banks of a small stream called the Rase, one of the sources of the River Ancholme.

Market Rasen is 13 miles south, south-east of Brigg, 16 miles north-east of Lincoln, 15 miles west of Louth, 20 miles east of Gainsborough and 149 miles north, north-west of London. It is in the centre of a fertile district, sheltered on the east and north by the Wolds. Running east and northeast is a geological belt known as blown sand, which produces heather, silver birches and conifers.

The West Lindsey council leaflet for the town, states, quote *"It is thought that the name 'Rasen' derived from raesn 'a plank"*" end of quote. What rubbish, hence the saying *"as thick as two short planks"* for who came up with that. Now let me tell you the true facts.

The name Rasen appears to signify upland waters, or high land streams and is derived thus: - Ra, meaning high, and Ouse, a stream. Its official designation is East Rasen. The spelling varied, and in the very early days, when just a collection of mud houses it was simply referred to as Rase. During the time of the Domesday Book it was referred to as Rase. In 1553 it was spelt Estereason. A decade later it was referred to as Estreason, which can be seen from the return made in 1563 to the Bishop of Lincoln by the Archdeacon: - Deanery, Walescrofte vicarage, Estreason, 64 families. The parish is within the Archdeaconry of Stow, and within the Rural Deanery of West Walescrofte...later this was spelt Walshcroft. This appears to indicate an early Welsh settlement, as may also the name of Walesby, a neighbouring village. In 1566 the spelling became Market Reason; in 1576 on an old map, it is shown as Merketrasin; in 1676, Market Raysin, alias East Raysin; while as late as 1850 the postal authorities have post-marked on the same envelope, Market Rasen, and the place of despatch West Raisen, [spelt as shown].

A certain John McCririck, who has something to do with horse racing, hence his knowledge of the town by way of its racecourse, calls the town … Market Raspberry, so keep up wind of him if you see him at Market Rasen races.

The following extract from the Domesday Book gives the names of some early landowners of Market Rasen in 1086:
Land of Roger of Poiton, Sokeland of this Manor in Rase, 8 ½ bovates, in Osgotebi 1 bovate, in Walesbi 1 carucate, in Otebi 1 carucate, there are 3 carucates and 1½ bovates of land (assessed) to the geld. There is land for 7 teams. There are 43 sokemen these having 4 teams and 60 acres of meadow and one mill rendering 3 shillings.

The 8 ½ bovates, held in 1086 by Roger of Poiton passed to the Earl of Mortain, under whom Roger de Mohtebegun was tenant.

Another reference gives more names of some of the owners of Market Rasen: *Manor Market Rasen Rolf had five bovates and three parts of a bovate of land rateable to geld. Wimund, the bishop's vassal, had one carucate and seven Villeins and three bordars with one carucate, and two mills worth 6 shillings annually and sixty-one acres of meadows.*

The Bishop's See was established at Lincoln in the year 1088, previous to which era, the diocess consisted of the two Anglo-Saxon Sees of Dorchester and Sidnacester, a place bordering on the River Trent. This latter See was established in 678 and was in and paramount over, the province of Lindsey. It had eighteen bishops, before Saint Remigius removed the See to Lincoln.

Connected with the cathedral and its ecclesiastical establishment, were the monasteries, hospitals and the like, which were very numerous, and some of great influence in this extensive district. The one near Market Rasen, just 4 miles east by south of the town was the Sixhills Priory, founded about the time of King Stephen., king of England from 1135 to 1154, by de Grelle of Greslie, an ancestor of Thomas de la Warre. It was for the Templars, a military order, founded in 1119, at the time of the crusades, by Huges de Payen and 8 other knights, to protect pilgrims from the attacks of the Saracens.

By Baldwin II, king of Jerusalem, they were granted quarters in his palace, built on the site of a temple, hence the name of the order.Their numbers rapidly increased and they became a powerful army, and acquired considerable wealth. Their income drawn from

European sources alone is estimated to have been about seven million pounds sterling. They adopted absolute secrecy to cover all their internal activities. King Philip the Fourth began to fear the Templars, and set about seeking their downfall. He accused them of heresy and immorality, and eventually succeeded in having Pope Clement the Fifth suppress the order on 22 March 1312, and two years later had the grand master, Jacques de Milay, burned at the stake. The Templars are known to be the ancestors of various groups, notably the Freemasons, for whom rites of initiation are important, and like the Knight Templars, they also adopt absolute secrecy to cover all their internal activities.

The various endowments of Sixhills Priory were confirmed to the nuns and brethren in the reign of King John - King of England from 1379 to 1390. It was a Gilbertine religious house inhabited by both nuns and monks. It was the only English order in the nation and took its name from Sir Gilbert de Semperingham, the eldest son of a Norman Knight, born in that village, and on taking Holy Orders he was presented to the churches of Sempringham and Tissington.

The monks followed the rules of Saint Augustine and the nuns those of Saint Benedict. One of their rules was that the monks should not see the nuns except at the administration of the Sacrament. The priory was dedicated to the Blessed Virgin and the monks and nuns followed the Sempringham rules. In this priory Edward the First confined Mary, the wife of Christopher Seton and sister of Robert Bruce, King of Scotland, in the year 1306. At the dissolution of the monasteries under Henry the Eighth its revenues were valued at £176.8s.9d per annum, and it was granted to Sir Thomas Heneage. Some of its remains may be seen in the house and outbuildings of the Grange Farm. Where the priory once stood are a few grass-covered mounds and one can still make out a pond.

The Charters which follow are from ' Transcript of Charters relating to Gilbertine houses' and refers to the priory of Sixhills and Market Rasen (East Rasen).

Charter I. (AD. 1135-1189. Stephen - Henry II)

"Be it known to all the faithful of Christ that I, Nicholas of Wadingham, have given and granted and by this my present charter confirmed, in pure and perpetual alms, to God and the Convent of Saint Mary of Sixle all my land and tenement in East Rasen (Estrasne) of the fee of Richard of Fleet, which William son of Hacon and Thomas his son held of me by heredity right, and their service,

which they did to me each year, namely half a mark of silver. Moreover I have made this gift and alms to them for the safety of my soul and the souls of my ancesters, which alms also I and my heirs will warrant to them against all men."

Charter II. (Henry the III AD 1216-1272).

"To all who shall see or hear this writing, Walter son of William of East Rasen sends greeting. Let the whole body of you know that I have granted and given to the convent of Sixle, the site of one grange to store their tithe, in my court which I hold of the same Convent by free service in the village of East Rasen (Hestrasyn) and free entry and exit for their waggons and carts through my court to the said grange without any hindrance of me or mine. Further, I have granted to the same convent and their tenants free entry and exit through my gate, to their own houses situated next the court to the east. And for the perpetual security of this matter I have seen fit to grant this writing, strengthened by my seal, to the same convent.

These being witnesses - Ralf, Vicar of Rasin; John of Claxslby; William of Bleseby; Walter, son of German de Mensaren; John, son of Thomas; William, son of Hamnor; Osbert, son of Thomas of Westrasyn; William his brother; Roger, son of William of Westrasyn."

CHAPTER 3

YOUNG GRACE

The Following names are as written in the records of the time … pronunciation maybe okay, but when one came to write the names of people and places, you must take into account that they would have had much more than just the odd bottle of vino de plonk … So let us continue, for it is important to see the names of people and places as written, and to see that Rasen had important property [possibly built on Roman sites] and people over a thousand years ago.

About 1150 Thomas of Saleby held the church and the mill at Market Rasen, and he gave them to Sixhills Priory. He left a young daughter, Grace who had a curious career. Her father was advanced in years [under statement] when she was born in 1194, and her uncle, the next heir, claimed that she was the child of peasants, and had been imposed on her father. The uncle lost his case, and on her father's death in 1199 she was married, at the age of 5, [yes, 5] to Adam de Nevill who died in 1201.

Within days, the king's chamberlain, Nicholas de Camera, gave 200 marks to marry Grace and have her lands. Nicholas also died in a few years, and in 1205 Brian de Lisle, a favourite with King John, paid 300 marks to the king for permission to marry Grace. De Lisle came from Dorsetshire and was governor of the castles of Bolsover and Knaresborough. When he died in 1234, Grace, now aged 40, at last got possession of her property, which included half a Knight's fee in East Rasen, held of the honour of Lancaster...at that period a Knight's fee consisted of land to the value of £20.

Grace now married Geoffrey de Worth, whom she may have chosen for herself. In 1250 Geoffrey and Grace granted to Robert, son of Jordan de Worth ... probably Geoffrey's nephew, the manors of East Rasen and Hainton, for the yearly rent of sixpence [definitely was Geoffrey's nephew at sixpence] or a pair of gilt spurs.

In 1259 Grace died and her cousin, William de Hardreshull, followed her. His son Robert succeeded in 1262, but was killed at the Battle of Evesham in 1265, fighting against the king. His estates were forfeited; Rasen and Hainton were given to Elias de Rabayne. Elias, already through his marriage with Matilda de Bayons, had the manors of Thoresway and Linwood, which had come down to her from Alfred of Lincoln.

Robert de Worth, who owned a manor in East Rasen, died in 1268. Isabel, wife of John Baron Vesey, held by way of rent, a property in Rasen which was formerly Alfred's which came to her brother, Henry Beaumont, Earl of Buchan, in 1331.

During this period, Grace's land in Rasen was divided into three parts, which were held as follows: -

1303, Roger de Croxby, Henry de Tyryngton, William de Mere.
1346, Robert de Breton, John Verdon, Robert de Worth.
1428, John de Thoresby, John Marbury, Prioress of Greenfield.

Of these owners, Tyryngton belonged to Torrington, the Bretons to Hatton and Panton. Greenfield nunnery bought their share in 1397. John Verdon belonged to Herefordshire. The Crophull's and Marbury's followed him. John Crophull of Weobley by Margery, daughter and co-heir of Theobald Verdon, had a son Thomas. Another Sir John Crophull held one third of the manor of Rasen at his death in 1384. Thomas's daughter Agnes, who held it in turn, married John Marbury and died in 1435. The relations are rather complicated, as her grandson by a former husband, Walter Devereux, married Elizabeth who was daughter and heir of John Marbury, by his first wife. It is not clear when their connection with Market Rasen ceased.

John de Thoresby lived at Croxby, and was probably descended from Roger de Croxby. The last John de Thoresby had an only daughter, Joan, who died in 1530, having married John Sheffield. The Sheffields of Croxby continued for several generations and are now remembered by the house Sheffield Manor [destined to be Miss Gledhill's School, but that is still many light years away]

The owners from this period of Market Rasen are not so easy to trace. Some valuable notes left by Lieutenant Colonel Conway Gordon [a military man would leave notes] show that one manor of Linwood, belonged to Alfred of Lincoln in 1005, and descended through the Bayons and Beaumonts down to 1500; and some land at Market Rasen went with it. During this period the church at Market Rasen began to get established. The parish registers for marriages begin in 1559, the first entry being: October 8, 1559, Willm Morton and Alce Baley. The first entry for baptisms was on October 6, 156l, Yssabell, dr of John Skyltone.

CHAPTER 4

MURDER AND RELIGIOUS UPRISING

During the Lincolnshire Uprising in 1537, men from Market Rasen played a large part in it. It became known as the Pilgrimage of Grace. Corruption had crept into the church during the Middle Ages; and, on top of that, the English Church, had embraced many errors. All these errors needed looking into, and a reformation...a very thorough cleansing in some points of faith and practice...was most imperative.

At the head of the nation was King Henry VIII (1509-1547) who ruled with a rod of iron. His principal adviser was Thomas Cromwell, who built Tattershall Castle and became known as 'the hammer of the monks'. He was a ruthless man, and on Henry's failure to gain the support of the papacy for his divorce and reorganisation of the Church of England, Cromwell suggested the plan of asserting the nation's religious autonomy and the king's supremacy over religious matters He thus effected passage of the Act of Supremacy (1534) and the confiscation of all monastic property by the crown.

On October 2, 1536, the king's commissioners for the suppression of the monasteries reached Caistor, where they learned that a great multitude from Louth were within a mile of the town, as well as crowds from Horncastle and Market Rasen. Mr Maddison and Mr Heneage were despatched to the king with a letter of complaint.

The uprising was only against the attempt to suppress the religious houses; it was not against the king or the church. Mackerel, Abbot of Barlings and a Suffragan Bishop; Nicholas Melton of Louth, shoemaker; Robert Youle and William Holton, priests of Louth; Master Thomas Kendall, B.D., vicar of Louth, were among the leaders. The commissioner's books were burned at Louth. Over 50,000 protestors congregated at Hambleton Hill just outside Market Rasen, and camped there on the night of Thursday, 5 October, before marching, via what is now Nova Scotia Bridge, along the byway [a BOAT that is now illegally blocked and should be open to the public] to come out at Caistor Road, opposite Gallamore Lane, which they headed down to Lincoln. Armed forces were sent against the angry multitude that offered to disband on condition of being pardoned.

The man who seemed to be in charge of the multitude was a shoemaker named Nicholas Melton, who immediately became known to everyone as Captain Cobbler. It ended with Captain Cobbler and the vicar of Louth being hanged at Tyburn. Thomas Moygne, a lawyer from Willingham, was hung, drawn and quartered for his involvement in the Lincolnshire Rising. The county had many religious houses and the people felt acutely the troubles that followed upon the Act of Suppression. To show how very thorough was the sweep made though Lincolnshire, which had nearly a hundred religious foundations, very few ruins remain, and many have been erased without a trace. In his letter to the rebels King Henry VIII described Lincolnshire as *"the most brute and beastly shire of the whole realm."*

The uprising effected Market Rasen for the Sixhills Priory had a strangle hold on the town by owning the church, mills and land. For over four hundred years Market Rasen came under the jurisdiction of the Sixhills Priory, and had paid tithes to that monastery during that period. Also, the Prioress of Greenfield, a priory of Cistercian nuns, founded before 1153 by Eudo de Greinesby and Ralph de Aby at Aby with Greenfield, about 3 miles north of Alford, owned one of the manors in East Rasen until the dissolution. At the time of the suppression there were about ten nuns at the convent whose gross revenues amounted to £79. 15s. 1d, and the Prioress of Greenfield was Joan Skipwith.

At East Rasen the people were by no means calm. And when it was found that the tithes of Saint Thomas's Church, given for over four hundred years to the Sixhills Priory, had been handed over to Richard Clarke, the people were out for blood, and Clarke was roughed-up. But Clarke survived the beating and he remained at East Rasen until he died in April 1556. Richard Clarke was a very rich man. He was listed as a yeoman, a landholder, with the status lower than a gentleman, and he left a large house in the town.

With the stranglehold eased, a few nuns and monks cast off their robes and abandoned their religion and settled in Market Rasen, one former nun being Isabel Wright from Sixhills Priory, who married the mercer John Burnesley. It is possible, that with a change of cloth, and the changes of worship in the parish church, she witnessed the burning of The Rood with Mary and John with the rest of the Images belonging to the Mass, in the town market place in 1563 in the presence of the parishioners and churchwardens, Thomas Rawlinson and Richard Cater.

At the beginning of Elizabeth's reign in 1558, the Mass book with all the rest of the same belonging to the papist service, was taken away by the queen's pursuivant, an officer named South, who had authority to do so, but it was not known what happened to it.

During 1565 and 1566, ornaments of the parish church were sold by the assent of the parishioners, and vestments were sold to Richard Rawlinson, Nicholas Boldon and Richard Chapman, but whether they were defaced or not, it is not known. Also, stoles, amice and linen appertaining to the popish service were sold to Isabel Houge.

During this period it is not possible to state the exact population of East Rasen, however, it is known that in 1539 West Rasen was able to supply forty able men for the wars...archers or bill men; Middle Rasen, forty-nine; while East Rasen supplied seventy-nine. In 1563 there were 64 families in East Rasen, which would give a total population of around 300.

Life of the town evolved around the market place with its shops, and by this period, the market had been moved from West Rasen to East Rasen, which had taken its place as the chief of the three Rasens. The doctor who served the three Rasens lived in East Rasen.

Mud, for mud bricks dried in the sun, was the chief building material for the houses that were thatched and some with stud walling. It is possible that some of the rich people may have had timber houses. It is doubtful if brick was yet available in any quantity, although the first true arch of sun-baked brick was made about 4000 BC in the ancient City of Ur.

The occupations of the town in the early 1600's were miller, tanner, tailor, draper, butcher, cook, mercer, servant, cordwainer, weaver, joiner, yeoman, husband man, shoemaker, glazier, candle maker and clergyman.

The main livestock appears to have been horses and cattle and most families had at least one horse. The mills were either wind or water driven. It is certain that one or two of the mills were horse driven, one horse-mill being owned by Richard Anderton.

Since the days of the Romans, Market Rasen has been the centre for the sale and slaughter of animals … horses, cattle, sheep, pigs, deer, for their meat and hides; and in the early expansion period of the early 1600's there were still plenty of oak trees and water; and, because that was so, top class tanners were attracted to the town.

The tanners of East Rasen were important, and a variety of clothes, boots and gloves were made in the town. One of the earliest known glove makers was John Farthyngton [no relation, not even a quarter relation]. A Thomas Lamkyn owned a candle house, tallow trough, and was a candle maker. He died in 1549.

By the late 1500's books were being sold in the town shops. These were mostly church books of the Anglican Church, psalms, and service. But from inventories of the period, copies of Aesop's Fables were listed. There were also Latin phrase books and a few classical books.

About this time a school, the forerunner of the De Aston Grammar School with having such as Latin phrase books and classical books, was established in the town. Nicholas Banks, who died in 1591, was described as usher to the school, and in his will, a total value of only £5 - 19s - 0d, he left books valued at £3 -13s - 0d. It is not possible to ascertain just what or where the school was, but there was definitely a school, and education had taken root in the town with many kinds of books, including hornbooks. In 1585 it was known that Doctor Henry Hooke, M.A., was schoolmaster of Market Rasen.

Kilnwell Road in the 1800's

There were quarrels, but few ever got out of hand; however, one quarrel did get out of hand … but did it? There was a quarrel in the market place between young Francis Cartwright and the Reverend William Storre, during which young Cartwright is said to have made threats, which caused Storre to seek the protection of the magistrates. To add salt in the wounds, Storre then preached a sermon that Cartwright thought was purposely aimed at him.

Ten days later, Cartwright saw Storre in Kilnwell Road [see photo] and attacked the clergyman with a dagger. It was early morning, and it was just a chance meeting. Storre died of his wounds. Cartwright was arrested and brought before the justice, where either for lack of the truth, or by the corrupt magistrate, or both, there was only token bail set, and once free on bail, Cartwright fled to France.

After young Cartwright fled to France, his father, who was one of the wealthiest residents of Market Rasen, obtained by producing the 'right' documents, a pardon for him from the king. Upon receipt of this news Cartwright returned to Market Rasen, married and then moved to Nettleton, a few miles north of Rasen.

Meanwhile, Storre's widow appealed against the pardon. But Cartwright was with friends, who had hushed up the incident. He felt secure now that he had married and settled down. He had two children who were baptised in 1609 and 1616 while he resided with his friend, Dr. Henry Hooke, rector of Nettleton, who a few years earlier had been vicar and school master at Market Rasen. He had married Ann Goodhand of Market Rasen and they had three children baptized there.

All was peaceful for many years, and the Storre incident forgotten. Then, one day during a quarrel - it was not said who started it - Cartwright fatally wounded a Mr Riggs at Grantham, and this time he was convicted of manslaughter and sent to prison for a year. When he came out it appears his family and friends deserted him, and without their help he was soon deeply in debt. To escape, he sailed as a volunteer under Sir Richard Hawkins against Algiers. But because he was continually fighting with other volunteers he was dismissed, and he was last heard of in 1621 when he returned to England.

William Storre, a native of Lincolnshire, was on May 25, 1597, presented by Queen Elizabeth to the vicarage of Market Rasen. Later, he became vicar of Aisthorpe, the place of his birth, but retained the office of Sunday Lecturer at Market Rasen where he was murdered. The date of the burial of the Reverend William Storre, as it stands in the Market Rasen Register, is 6th September 1602.

Now let us look at the other side of the coin, which will explain why Storre was attacked. At the time William Storre was attacked, and died from his wounds, he was deep in debt, owing money to two mercers in Lincoln and to a draper in London. There could have been many others; and, this could have been why he was murdered for he had been pressed for the money.

In 1634, Gentry in Lincolnshire, that is, those persons who were entitled to use a coat of arms...were two people from Market Rasen; Robert Fitche and John Wright. It is possible that they were in battle with them a decade later, for during the Civil War...1642 to 1651, the conflict between King Charles I and parliament, Market Rasen was raided by the Royalists in 1644. Lincolnshire as a county was more for parliament than for King Charles and the cavaliers. After the battle of Winceby, Oliver Cromwell moved from Horncastle via Market Rasen to Gainsboro. Cromwell, an East Anglian cavalry leader, fought and won the main battles, one being at Marston Moore [1644] where he defeated Prince Rupert. A parliamentary victory resulted in the king's execution.

During this period many Tradesman's Tokens came into being and at Market Rasen. William Chapman issued his Half Peny; reverse, of Market Reason, W.C. 1666. The size of the token was slightly smaller than a sixpence. Mr. Thies in 1927 found one on the golf links, Willingham Road, in very good condition.

There is in the Lincoln museum a farthing token of the 17th century, issued by William Blowe of Market Rasen. Obverse: - William Blowe, shield, the Grocer's Arms; reverse: - In Market Reason, W.A.B.

The 1676 Census at Market Raysin, alias East Raysin, was 199 conformists, 1 non-conformist, 20 papists; 220 inhabitants above 16 years of age. Traders and shops had increased, and as its wealth increased, so did the appearance of the town. Glaziers were now in demand as ownership of glass windows was now commonplace. First reference to glass windows in the town was in 1575, but this was only for the wealthy. Luxury goods now began to appear.

CHAPTER 5

THE ENCLOSURES IN 1779

In the 17th century Linwood belonged to the Caesar family, beginning with Sir Julius Adelmare, alias Caesar, Master of the Rolls. About 1700, Linwood, with part of Market Rasen, came into the hands of Samuel Shepperd of Exning, near Newmarket, whose only daughter, Frances, married in 1756, Charles, 9th Viscount Irvine. Lady Irvine had no sons but she did have five daughters who became her heirs, one of whom, the honourable Frances Ingram-Sheppard became the wife of Lord William Gordon, a younger son of the Marquess of Huntly and was lady of the manor of Market Rasen and Linwood. The Conway- Gordon family followed her for a long period.

Other notable families who have owned land in Market Rasen include the Monsons, Nelthorpes, Moignes of North Willingham and Booths of Killingholme, one being a vicar.

The connexion with the Duchy of Lancaster, which occurs as early as 1250, still existed after 1700, when the sale of some houses in Pinfold Street (now Oxford Street) was recorded in the court of the Duchy.

The church has always been landowner and a Terrier is a record of land and other property belonging to the vicar of the parish. Information giving details of early Market Rasen Terriers extracted from the registry of the Lord Bishop of Lincoln, as follows:

Dated 1707: A Terrier of East Rasen alias Market Raisen vicarage in ye Deanery of Walshcroft and archdeaconry of Lincoln given at Michaelmas - Visitation at Caister 1707.

The vicarage house is made of clay, walls floored with brick and covered with straw there are 3 rooms below and as many chambers and joins to ye churchyard and stands west of ye church there is no out-house but one small stable of one bay ye house yards and churchyard contain near two acres ye churchyard is fenced with rails ye other yards with hedges. There is no glebe nor any close but there are four small houses in ye market place West of ye market which belong to ye Vicarage containing six bayes of building walled and floored with clay and covered with straw.

In 1709 there was a major disaster at Market Rasen but it is very difficult to determine the cause or actual damage. From the church records of Upper Boddington, Northamptonshire, it does show that there were two fires at Market Rasen. One was 15 May 1709 and another 16 September 1711 and figures stated being £1228 and £1169; but it is impossible to furnish more evidence or to say whether these two briefs refer to the same event or if Market Rasen had a double disaster. However, it is clear that from the sums named the extent of the damage must have been somewhat considerable.

From Speculum Dioeceseos it is known that at Market Rasen between 1705 and 1723 there were 120 families, five papists and four anabaptists. The town was growing. The vicar of that period was Mr. Francis Smith, resident from 1692; he was also vicar of Croxby and curate of Middle Rasen Tupholm. A lectureship with stipend of £20, or £16 per annum.

In March 1732, Thomas and Isaac Hallam were executed for murder. The former hung in chains on a gibbet. Bodies were permitted to hand on gibbets, as a salutary warning to passers-by, and the gibbets were just before the turning into Lincoln Lane [still the main A46] to Middle Rasen; the latter near Bunker's Hill toll bar, on the Nettleham Road, where the murder was committed.

In 1733 it was decided to stop using Latin in the registers. That same year there were 31 burials entered, of which 20 were infants. Surely there must have been a fatal epidemic raging at this time. The following year there were 28 burials entered, of which 16 were infants. This was still a very high figure for the size of the population.

The open field system was about to end; this was done at Middle Rasen in 1774, at Market Rasen in 1779. However, even before this date of 1779, some local enclosure had already taken place around the church and the open land before it, which became known as the market place. The right to hold a market at Market Rasen goes right back to 1219.

Because of these early enclosures at Market Rasen, which included a mill close, it made it a more convenient place for the changing of horses. This was a very useful start for the growing town and shows it as a centre for service and mobility. Market Rasen had the advantage over the villages.

At the time of the enclosure the main people who got three acres or more of the 730 Market Rasen acres was as follows: Albany Wallis, 272 acres; Rev. Thomas Nocton, 89 acres; Thomas Wright, 34 acres; John Scott, 24 acres; George Tennyson, 21 acres; George

Shuttleworth, 14 acres; William Hollingworth, 13 acres; Edward Howith, 8 acres; Joseph Kendall, 7 acres; Thomas Parratt, 6 acres; Joseph Robinson, 6 acres; Richard Carter, 6 acres; Henry Booth, 5 acres; John Scott (as trustee), 5 acres; John Flintham, 5 acres; John Johnson, 4 acres; Rev. John Robinson, 4 acres; Thomas Houghton, 3 acres; Dorothy Sallitt, 3 acres; John Cousins, 3 acres; Catherine Brooke, 3 acres; Sarah Rowlands, 3 acres; Benjamin Plaskitt, 3 acres; James Neve and Hellen Jones, 3 acres. In addition there were 23 allotments of smaller areas and altogether there were 97 parcels of land awarded to 47 separate owners, and the man with the lions share was Albany Wallis, who in addition to his direct grant of 272 acres which, was roughly a third of the parish, he also received four acres in lieu of his manorial rights. It was obvious Wallis had the Enclosure Commissioners in his pocket for he must have been an important man, who was out for a quick killing for he had little or no interest in Market Rasen. Compared to Wallis's lion share, 1 acre, 3 roods, 35 perch of land was allotted to the surveyors of the highways and part of it was a gravel pit. The enclosure was the end of an era for Market Rasen and the surrounding countryside.

After the enclosures, a revolution occurred in farming techniques and up to that time there hadn't been much difference in size and population between any of the three Rasens. Market Rasen was in fact smaller than Tealby, which had so many mills, including a flourishing paper mill.

CHAPTER 6

THE BATTLE OF WATERLOO

During the wars with France, in Napoleon's day, there was from time to time fear of an invasion. At the Battle of the Nile in August 1798, Nelson destroyed the French fleet, and in so doing, cut off Napoleon's Egyptian expedition from its base, so ending the threat to British interests in India.

But in March 1799, Napoleon defeats the Turks at Jaffa, and in July of that year, defeats the Turks and British at Abukir.

Market Rasen was along way from the fighting, but many additional troops were raised because of the Napoleonic Wars. The ordinary North and South Lincoln Mililitia was increased in strength; and Brigg, Caistor and Market Rasen also combined to form a regiment in the body of Loyal Lincoln Volunteers in 1803.

Eleven troops of Yeomanry cavalry were raised in Lincolnshire, among which Market Rasen came forward in 1797.The troop numbered usually between 40 and 60 men under the command of a captain, lieutenant and cornet.

The earliest reference discovered is from the diary of the Reverend John Robinson, rector of Faldingworth: *'On Thursday, Nov 8th 1798,the Market Rasen troop of Yeomanry Cavalry was mustered on the lawn at Willingham, when in the presence of a very large company...the Colours being previously there consecrated by the Reverend T. J. Holme, the chaplain to the troop, were presented by desire of Mrs Boucherett (who had herself worked them) by Colonel Maddison. The Troop and sundry gentleman afterwards dined at Mrs Boucherett's at Willingham. On Thursday, June 4th, 1799, being the king's birthday, I dined with the Market Rasen troop, who unanimously chose me their chaplain, on Mr Holme's quitting the curacy of Market Rasen.'*

On 11 June 1799, the Rasen cavalry joined the Alford Infantry and the Louth Independent Yeomanry at Louth Market Place at 10 a.m. for the presentation of Colours to the Loyal Louth Infantry. They proceeded to the church where the vicar preached and consecrated the Colours, which were afterwards presented to the captain by Mrs Colonel Loft in uniform.

Orders were sent out as follows: *"The Market Rasen Cavalry are required to muster at Head Quarters on Monday 21st inst at 11 o'clock to be inspected by Lieutenant-Colonel Anderson. The clothes and portmanteaus are expected to be well brushed and the horses well trimmed before they appear on parade."*

J. Elliott, cornet, 18 March 1808. From the diaries of Thomas John Dixon of Holton-le-Moor, who joined the troop in 1802 and rose to become its captain, it is clear that the dinner on the king's birthday was a regular event until George III's death in 1820 and even for a year or two after on April 23. It was held at different inns in turn.

Mr Ayscoghe Boucherett also entertained the troop in November for several years. He was Lt-Col of the whole corps of Lincolnshire Yeomanry and died in 1815. Some troops went away for periods of training, but at Market Rasen the required number of days were made up at intervals throughout the year.

At the Battle of Trafalgar, which was fought on 21 October 1805, west of Cape Trafalgar, Spain, between Cadiz and the straight of Gibraltar. A fleet of 33 ships -18 French and 15 Spanish - under Admiral Pierre de Villeneuve, fought a British fleet of 27 ships under Admiral Horatio Nelson.

This naval engagement of the Napoleonic wars, which established British naval supremacy for more than 100 years, ended the already weakened possibility of a French invasion of England.

In 1814 France was defeated and Napoleon was exiled to the island of Elba. The next year he returned to France and regained power [for the period known as the hundred days] until defeated at Waterloo by the British [under the Duke of Wellington] and the Prussians.

The horse, which the Duke of Wellington rode at the Battle of Waterloo on Sunday 18 June 1815, was born and bred at Market Rasen. The horse was named Copenhagen and the Duke of Wellington rode the horse for 18 hours. It had rained all night. The men had not slept and were soaked through. The food supplies were deficient on both sides, which meant that the soldiers would have to fight all day on empty stomachs. The battle was fought three miles (five kilometres) south of Waterloo village, which is nine miles south of Brussels, Belgium. Napoleon had 72,000 men plus 246 cannons. The Duke of Wellington's Allied army totalled 67,700 men plus 156 cannons, made up as follows: English 24,000, Belgo-Dutch 17,800, Hanovians 11,300, Brunswickians 6,000, Royal German Legion 5,800 and the Dutch of Nassau 2,800 men. Wellington also had

52,500 Prussians plus 135 cannons, the main force of Gebbard Leberecht von Blucher's command.

Napoleon made a major blunder in delaying his attack on Wellington from morning until 11.30 a.m., his reason being to allow- the ground to dry, but this delay gave Blucher's troops exactly the time they needed to reach Waterloo and support Wellington.

At about 4.0 p.m. Marshal Michel Ney thought he saw the English centre fall back and he decided the time had come to throw in his large cavalry force. Thus started the fantastic charge, which was to last two hours and exhaust the French cavalry. The cavalry made successive charges against the Allied squares, which stood firm against this avalanche and stopped it from reaching the plateau. These wild charges, without precedent in military history, were made without infantry.

At 8.15 p.m. the general allied advance began and for Napoleon the battle was lost. They fought to the last man and few escaped. Wellington's Army was too exhausted to continue beyond Rosomme Farm, and the Prussian cavalry undertook the chase alone, as the French forces retreated from Waterloo across the River Loire.

Napoleon lost 42,000 men. Wellington's casualties were 16,000 and Blucher's were about 7,000 men. After 18 hours Wellington dismounted and patted his horse with great affection, the latter showed his mettle by playfully flinging up his heels into the air, as fresh as though he had only been out for half-an-hour's exercise. It had been a ferocious battle, but it was equally glorious for all. Copenhagen died aged 27 at Strathfieldsaye in Hampshire, and was buried with military honours.

Before the Battle of Waterloo, from 13 to 20 days a year was fixed for mustering the Market Rasen Yeomanry Cavalry, but after peace was declared only five to eight days was necessary. The troop was kept to the level of efficiency by frequent inspections; between 1805 and 1812 there were always two a year and sometimes four. The inspecting officer was frequently Lord Yarborough's brother, Colonel Anderson or Colonel Ainslie, who was a cousin of Mrs Heneage.

Men were enrolled in the troop from many parishes as far off as Bishop Norton, Grasby, South Willingham and Spridlington. It was customary to choose their own officers, who were then confirmed by commission from the Lord Lieutenant. These included: - Captains A Boucherett, junr, resigned 1817, T J Dixon, 1817.

Lieutenants- Shuttleworth [probably Dr George Shuttleworth] buried with military honours 19 Nov 1806. Francis Otter, died 1813. J H Vane 1817. Samuel Cropper 1824. Cornets John Elliott, T J Dixon 1809, J H Vane 1813, S Cropper 1817. Quartermaster John Lancaster, shoemaker.

Thomas Marmaduke Young was also an officer. A Boucherett, junior, was born in 1791, so possibly it was his father who was the first captain. In the early days of the troop there are payments to the barber for hair powder on the muster days. The government provided arms, ammunition and a small allowance towards clothes.

T.J. Dixon's helmet and epaulettes were given to the Lincoln Museum.

Not all troops were cavalry, and in 1804 there was a rifle and carbine section, but the regular arms were sword and pistol. In 1817 the captain applied to the ordnance office for leave to increase the establishment from 57 to 68; he also asked for 20 new pistols or sword belts, as the arms had been in use for nearly 20 years and were becoming unfit for service.

In the later days of the troop a contingent allowance was made by the War Office of 30 shillings a head to encourage efficient members. Men were fined for non-attendance. An earlier allowance from the government amounted to £6 - 9s - 2d for two years. The uniform included, jacket with trimmings complete £3- 3s, saddle £3 - 3s, bridle £1-10s, leather helmet £1-16s, leather breeches £1-16s, holster £1- 1s, waistcoat 16s, slip coat case 12s -3d, besides smaller items. The troop continued for thirty years but on 17 December 1827, orders were received for disbanding. On 13 February 1828, the captain gave orders at Market Rasen for the arms to be packed and sent to the ordnance depot at Hull, and on 6 May, the accounts were wound up and the quartermaster paid in full. This was not however the end of Market Rasen's connection with yeomanry; in 1831 the New North Lincoln Yeomanry included two Rasen names. Lieutenant Z Barton and Ensign George Saffery. I am certain that the Barton, is Doctor Zechariah Barton of Sheffield Manor.

Market Rasen was remembered for its part in the Napoleonic War for on a window of the White Hart Hotel, there was, evidently by the use of a diamond, an inscription to the following effect: *"Turn us, 0 God, and we shall be turned."* Under these words, a drawing of an ornamental cup with a monogram of the letters B.T.S., and the date 11th March 1814. On the next pane the words: *"Prepare to meet your God,"* and the signature Col O'Dinner. It was thought that this was the work of two officers of the 14th Hussars, when they stayed in Market Rasen on their way from York to Boston, en route for France to engage in the war with Napoleon, which resulted in the memorable victory at Waterloo.

Waterloo Road [when first named] derives its name from the Battle of Waterloo; yet, no mention of the fact that Copenhagen, the horse that Duke of Wellington rode at the Battle of Waterloo, was bred at Market Rasen. Not a mention from the town council. His horse so named because Wellesley (Duke of Wellington) was at the bombardment of Copenhagen in 1807, and arranged the conditions of the surrender of the Danes. So he named his horse, Copenhagen.

For 1822, the following information, extracted from the Registry of the Lord Bishop of Lincoln, gives more information about a Terrier of Market Rasen:

A true note and Terrier of all the glebes, lands, meadows, gardens, orchards, houses, stocks, implements, tenements, portions of tithes and other rights, belonging to the vicarage and parish church of Market Rasen in July 1822.

One brick and tiled dwelling house in length 38ft 10in in breadth 14ft 6in within the walls and office adjoining. One brick and tiled stable, one court yard south of the house, one garden north of the house, four tenements with gardens adjoining. Also three shops situate on the west side of the Market Place. Also six other shops adjoining the south end, all, which said tenements and gardens, contain two roods and twenty-seven perches.

The churchyard containing two roods and eighteen perches bounded on the west by the vicarage house and garden on the north and east by the Castor Road and, on the south by dwelling houses belonging to Lord William Gordon and Ann Clark, the walls and gates thereof on the east and north made by the parish, and the west by the vicar.

One piece or parcel of glebe land in the high field containing thirty-seven acres three roods and thirty-six perches, which said allotment, was formerly thirty-nine acres three roods and thirty-six perches. Two acres being sold off to redeem the land tax, the said glebe has been sub-divided into six fields with good quick hedges.

One other allotment of glebe land in the Middle Carr containing fifty three acres three roods and seventeen perches now divided into three fields and bounded on south by the road leading to North Willingham as described in the award.

For the tithe of mills, maltkilns and tanyards six shillings and eightpence each collected yearly at Midsummer.

There is also belonging to the said Parish one Inclosure called the Church Meadow containing twelve acres one rood and eight perches which is bounded on the North by the Louth Road and on the East and South by land of Lord William Gordon and on the West by land of Mary Ann Shuttleworth, the fence on the North and East made by the Parish on the South by Lord William Gordon and on the West by Mary Ann Shuttleworth, the rent of which is applied for extraordinary repairs of the parish church

(Signed) James Walter, vicar of Market Rasen.
James Clark and John Slater - Churchwardens.

The above is a true copy of a Terrier given at the Bishop's Visitation on 17 July 1822. The above does name who had land and where. It also shows that the mills, malt kilns and tan-yards were in full swing, the latter increasing, hence the need for more tanners.

CHAPTER 7

THE 1800's

Town Hall and market place

The Town Hall and market place is where the town started. Note the name Nettleship on the Town Hall, for the Nettleship Family destined to be a key player in the town, but not always for the town. Note also the gas lamp on stone pedestal on the right, for reference to this later. The Town Hall gave Market Rasen much of its personality, but brown envelopes here, and brown envelopes there, and it is gone. Why was it not preserved?

In the early days there were two roads passing through Rasen, the main one was the one running west to east through West and Middle Rasen, and going on through East Rasen, and Willingham towards Louth. This main road, which formed the main street of the town, was crossed by another from Wragby, which went in the direction of Tealby and Binbrook. A few rambling offsets north and south led into the fields, soon to change into ling, prickly gorse, stretches of pine wood and amber sand.

Bogs were numerous in many parts of Lincolnshire and a Mr.Young remarked *"Bogs are so numerous, that he is a desperate fox-hunter, who ventures to ride here without being well acquainted with the ground. I have rarely seen a county that wants exertions in draining more than this. Many similar springy sides of hills are to be met with all the way to Ranby, and thence by Oxcomb to Louth."*

The year was 1800, and at that period, land had a value of about 5 shillings an acre, some much less, and after one hundred and fifty thousand acres had been drained, its value rose to £1 - 5s per acre.

Within a few years Market Rasen had eleven private roads. The first seven were Legsby Road, Pasture Road, Lammas Leas Road, Bellamy's Road, Mill Road, Kilnwell Road and Jack Lane Road. The other four were occupation roads, which had to be maintained by the owners of lands who used the roads. These were Albany Wallis's Road, Richard Chappel's Road, George Tennyson's Road and Charles Plasket's Road.

Market Rasen typified exactly the new kind of service centre, which came into being. But up to about the time of the 1790's, it was not anything like certain that Market Rasen would be the centre to grow. It could have been Caenby, on the road between Rasen and Gainsborough. The Caenby Corner Inn, known as the Moncks Arms, provided a very convenient place for the changing of horses, and it was a good place for starting off on a journey to London. Caenby was very much favoured as a new North Lincolnshire market centre. At that period Charles Tennyson lived at Caenby Hall.

But a new turnpike road was built running from Bawtry to Louth, and the White Hart Hotel, at Market Rasen, owned and run by Mrs Smith, an astute business Lady, who was destined to play a major role in the birth of the town, provided a good changing point for horses on this road. Mrs Smith knew that stagecoaches made towns. The White Hart had plenty of good stables, rooms for travellers and good public rooms. Mrs Smith had all the right facilities, including plenty of good ostlers – men who groom horses, for the horse was very important, for no horses, no stage coaches. Let us remember, at this period Rasen was still mostly open space on which roamed animals. The population little more than 600. The coachmen of the day were the key, and Mrs Smith knew it. She gave good vibes for business, thus Rasen attracted blacksmiths, shopkeepers and other people who provided a foundation for rural trade. What was happening was the birth of a new farming pattern with a little town coming into being just to serve the villages, and to market and transport the corn and other produce from the land.

The houses in the main street of Market Rasen presented a series of gaps. Those in the market place in the early 1800's were mostly roofed with thatch. The foot pavement, surfaced with hard pebbles, was purgatory to tender feet. The resident ladies who ventured out shopping, either to the emporiums of James Bond or John Morley in Dear Street, generally wore clogs on their feet, and entrancing coalscuttle bonnets on their heads.

Top photo is George Street and below is East House

The oldest houses then existing were two in George Street [see photograph, the two thatched cottages on the left], the Greyhound Inn [1560], the oldest in the area, and East House [1650] on Willingham Road. The thatch was taken off in 1889. In the early days was called 'Half-Way House' and the owners made and repaired carts. The forge was at the back of the house. A wheel right was on hand for breakdowns, like an early AA service.

Various industries [now vanished] were carried on by John Northing, the weaver; George Turtle, leather breeches and gloves; Mr Dexter, gunsmith; Mr G Walker, fellmonger; Samuel Cropper kept stables for thorough-bred hunters and hacks; John and Charles Clarke carried on the business of candle making in John Street. The Clarke's were also drapers, grocers, farmers and unregistered bankers. Mr George Spencer Watkinson, born in Hull, was a pipe maker in Serpentine Street, and was the only one remaining by the 1850's. The clay for his pipes came from Devon, by sea and canal to Gainsborough, and then by road.

Not just Market Rasen, but also the whole country was moving forward. In general terms England was advancing to victory against the French, and at Market Rasen the squires rubbed their hands as their rent rolls suddenly increased.

In the Market Rasen area the nearest squire was Ayscough Boucherett, who was building Willingham House, just at the same time as the Rasen enclosure inquiry was proceeding. Willingham House, standing less than two miles east from Market Rasen was a stylish example of Georgian countryside building. Its Ionic portico and massive pillars bespoke confidence of a whole class.

A new lake was brought into being between the mansion and the turnpike road running from Market Rasen to Louth. The neo-classical mansion did not bring happiness for the Boucherett family, and the greatest tragedy came in 1832, when the central pole of his two-wheeled chaise, drawn by two horses, snapped as they were descending Willingham Hill and Ayscough Boucherett was killed instantly when he was thrown out and hit his head.

At the time of the 1818 election, Market Rasen seemed to be without any manufacturing industry, but on the other hand it was laying the foundation as a major rural service centre. Rasen had blacksmiths, shoemakers, butchers, bricklayers and increasing all the time. It was springing up with incredible buoyancy and was establishing itself as the top place of the district. Rasen offered genuine opportunities for the adventurous and even for those who were just in search of a secure place to work.

From 1814 to 1824, the Reverend Matthew Barnett was curate of Market Rasen, and he established masonry in Lincolnshire as early as 1787. In 1793 he was elected to the dignity of D.P.G.M. by which time several Lodges were formed. The whole management of the craft of the county devolved upon him in his official capacity, and it appears, owing in great measure to his exertions, that masonry took on the cloak of respectability. He received the public thanks of the congregated Masons of Lincolnshire at fourteen P.G. Lodges, which he personally attended. The Reverend Matthew Barnett died in 1833, and was buried in the Parish Church in Market Rasen. There is a Tablet to his memory in the North Aisle.

Over the River Rase, at the start of Caistor Road

In 1821 the Market Rasen parish contained 243 houses and 1166 inhabitants. With the continued expansion of the town a new bridge was built in 1832 over the River Rase, at the start of Caistor

Road. It is constructed of brick and stone with iron palisades. The span of the arch is twenty feet, and the roadway twenty-two feet. The cost was £613, and Mr. J.S. Padley was the architect and the builder. The contractor was Mr. John Broadgate. Two smaller bridges, one in Waterloo Road and the other in Jameson Bridge Street, were erected in 1853 and 1855 at a cost of about £200 each.

A Mechanics' and Literary Institute was established in Union Street in 1836 with about 600 volumes and 100 members. The aim of the Mechanics' Institute was primarily to educate mechanics. There were monthly lectures, and in 1851 a class to study grammar was formed, and later classes in writing and arithmetic. The Mechanics' Institute had a good supply of weekly papers and the Times were also available.

The Mechanics' Institute had the backing of many prominent people, and these included, Angerstein Boucherett of Willingham House. The Honourable C.A. Pelham, son of the Earl of Yarborough, and C.E. Heanage of Hainton Hall. Therefore, it was not surprising that in 1851 the Mechanics' Institute sponsored the opening of the Penny Savings Bank. However in 1858 the Penny Savings Bank called in all the depositors books in order that they could be balanced, after the many rumours that things were not as they should be.

The Mechanics' Institute also had the cloth amongst its supporters, and in 1851, the Reverend G.S. Scobell was their Vice President. During his time he gave many lectures, two being of particular interest... *'The Life and Character of the Duke of Wellington,' and 'The Poetry and Prose of War.'*

The secretary in 1872 was Mr William Marshall, and by 1885 the Mechanics' Institute and Library had moved to rooms in Queen Street, and at that time, Sanderson Naylor was librarian.

Bayon's Lodge of Freemasons, No. 1286, met in the Corn Exchange, the first Monday in every month during this period. Though often mistaken for such, freemasonry is not a Christian institution. For admission the applicant is required to be an adult male, believing in the existence of a Supreme Being and in the immortality of the soul. In practice, some lodges have been charged with prejudice against Jews, Catholics, and non-whites. Freemasonry has, almost from its inception, encountered considerable opposition from organized religion. Freemasonry is banned in the former Union of Soviet Republics, Hungary, Poland, Spain, Portugal, China, Indonesia, the United Arab Republic and elsewhere.

Like the Knight Templars, the freemasons also adopt absolute secrecy to cover all their internal activities. They have an initiation ceremony and the recruit has to be dressed in black silk pyjamas. Not all members can stay to see it. All members wear white gloves, and their book of rules is coded in case it falls into outsiders hands. The dark world of the freemasons took root in Market Rasen.

In 1831 gas was introduced into the town. The gas works were erected at the cost of £1650, raised by 15 shareholders, but they were later enlarged and improved. The gas works became another of the town's growing industries.

There was steady progress with the installation of gaslights for the town, and by December 1850, it was decided there should be seven more; one in Serpentine Road, one at the bottom of Prospect Place and Mr. Neave's corner in Willingham Street, one in Oxford Street, one in Waterloo Road, one in Dear Street and two in Union Street. The town's gaslights were only allowed to burn until mid-night, whereas, in many other towns at that period, they were allowed to burn all night. Also, Market Rasen gas was much dearer than other towns, for example, the Market Rasen Gas Company charged private consumers, the exorbitant sum of 10 shillings per 1000 feet, whereas in other towns it was about half that sum.

The towns' people were outraged at the high gas prices and called many meetings but it got them nowhere. Meanwhile, the gas company continued to lay new pipes. But during the winter of 1855-56, the supply of gas was insufficient for the needs of the town. The talking to get the gas price reduced, continued, but their calls for a reduction fell on deaf ears. To show some good faith, the directors of the Gas Company decided to raise the market place lamp on a stone pedestal, about 3 feet high and 5 feet square at the base and to also provide a much better burner for the lamp. This was carried out in early 1859 [see photo at start]. In 1860 two more street lamps were erected in Willingham Street, two on Walesby Road and one in Church Street.

Three very neat Roman Catholic almshouses were erected at the west end of the town on the Gainsborough Road in 1841, pursuant to the will of the late David Young of West Rasen, who died in 1832, and who bequeathed an endowment of £20 yearly to each of the three inmates, who also lived rent free. The houses bear the inscription *'Of your charity pray for the founder, David Young. May his soul rest in peace.'*

The terrace of almshouses in Caistor Road were built in 1620, and endowed by Sir George Saint Poll of Snarford, the same knight who had founded a hospital at Market Rasen in 1612. This Knight and Baronet came from a very ancient family, dating from the reign of King Stephen (1135-1154). John Saint Paule...also written 'Sanctpoll', 'Pole' and 'Poll', married the daughter and heiress of John de Snarford, whose estate passed into the Saint Paule family in the reign of Edward III. From this John Saint Paule descended George Saint Paule of Snarford, who married in 1583 Frances Wray, second daughter of Christopher Wray, Lord Chief Justice of England.

Lady Saint Poll, who in the same year her husband died, married (as his second wife) Robert, Baron Rich of Leeze, created Earl of Warwick, 6 August 1618. (There is an inscription in Snarford Church).

As Countess of Warwick, she erected the hospital for eight poor people at Market Rasen, with an endowment of £40 per annum charged on the Faldingworth estate. The countess added to its endowment an annuity of £7- 4s- 0d out of land at Buslingthorpe. Only half of the alms people resided in the hospital, the other four were non-resident pensioners. Three of them belonged to Market Rasen, the other five were chosen, one from each of the following parishes, Welton, Snelland, Legsby, Faldingworth and Snarford. Each person was given 1s- 6d per week; blue coats every second year, and a gratuity at Christmas.

The sum of £120, left by Sir George Saint Poll to the poor of Market Rasen, was laid out, with £10, given by Christopher Naylor in 1665, in the purchase of land at Tealby. In the 1850's this land was let for £28 per year.

Lady Frances Countess Dowager of Warwick in 1625 gave for the benefit of the poor of this parish, a cottage and garden at Middle Rasen, to which three acres were allotted at the enclosure, and in the 1850's produced £18 per annum. At this time they also had a 20 shillings yearly rent charge out of Polcher's Close in Linwood; another 15 shillings out of Crane Bridge Close; and one of 20 shillings left by William Osney, out of an estate belonging in 1856 to J. Tateson, and the vicar.

CHAPTER 8

THE MID 1800's

Middle Rasen Road

Seeing that the next paragraph mentions the birds and the bees, what better way to open the chapter than by a lovely view of the west side of the town? What a lovely, romantic view of Middle Rasen Road that greets people to Market Rasen.

The first census of Great Britain was made in 1801 and it is interesting to note that from the 1851 census, two Market Rasen women were listed under the oldest profession in the world, one aged 48, the other 11... obviously learning the art.

By the mid-1800's Market Rasen was beginning to boom, and there were a great variety of trades and crafts practised in the town. To accommodate the increasing need for knowledge there were now two booksellers in the town; John Gilbert Caborn, who was listed as stationer, engraver, printer and stamp office; and Richard Hackett, also listed as engraver, printer and paperhanger.

One flourishing business in the 1850's was insurance. But this was nothing new as insurance in some form, has been used as long as man has lived in historical society. Merchants of Babylon knew so-called bottomry contracts as early as 4,000-3000 BC. The Hindus also practiced bottomry in 600 BC and in ancient Greece as early as the 4th century BC. Ancient Roman law recognized the bottomry contract, in which an article of agreement was drawn up and funds were deposited with a moneychanger.

In Rome there were also burial societies that paid funeral costs of their members out of monthly dues. The insurance contract also developed very early. It was known in ancient Greece, and among other maritime nations in commercial contact with Greece. The mention of other maritime nations is due to the fact, that bottomry means the practice of borrowing money, on the security of a ship. Fire insurance came much later, obtaining impetus from the Great Fire of London in 1666. Insurance companies mushroomed overnight; many of them were fraudulent, get-rich-quick schemes. Nevertheless, two important and successful English insurance companies were formed during this period...the London Assurance Corporation and the Royal Exchange Assurance Corporation. They marked the beginning of modern property and liability insurance. So, it was not surprising that Market Rasen had fourteen insurance agents.

Also to flourish in the 1850's with the increase of population were the Friendly Societies, and at that time there were at least nine in Market Rasen. They served a valuable need and the financial help was most welcome in times of sickness or to the family with bereavement. But, also important was the support of the fellowship during the time of need.

There were also two burial clubs, the Philanthropic Funeral Society and the King's Head Funeral Society; two local lodges of Oddfellows, the Boucherett Lodge of the Nottingham Imperial Order and the Heart of Honesty Lodge of the Manchester Unity. Others were the Shepherdess Friendly Society, the Lodge of the Order of the Ancient shepherds of the Ashton Unity and the Infant Shepherds.

After long hours at work, the people of Market Rasen knew how to enjoy themselves, and during the mid-1800's one favourite pastime was the Shrove Tuesday football. Just about all the male population of the town took part, aided by their friends from outside, and they spent many strenuous hours in trying to get the ball into Middle Rasen. The windows were boarded-up all along the road, and the struggle of hundreds of boisterous fellows, well tanked with Rasen Ale, was more concerned in pushing their opponents into the beck by the roadside than in keeping on the ball.

Other forms of recreation for the children were climbing the grease pole in the market place, tag, foot races, and wheelbarrow races or, just making their own enjoyment in the countryside. In those days children knew how to make do with the simple things in life.

Fetes were held at Bayons Manor, the home of Tennyson d'Eyncourt, and at Willingham Hall. People also looked forward to the annual feast of the town, and for the children, the annual Sunday school outings. All were very much enjoyed. During the spring fair there was a hiring day for servants.

During this time, horse races were held in the last week of September, and steeplechases in March. The horses were those of gentlemen mostly from the Brocklesby and Burton Hunts. The races were held on the Caistor Road side of the town. The first recorded race meeting at Market Rasen was on Thursday the 17th March 1859.

The poor also had their leisure pursuits, the most popular being cock-fighting and rat catching with terrier dogs. Whippet racing was also popular, and a few kept pigeons as pets, but many times they ended up in the pot.

Next to dog and cock fighting came the simple pleasure of getting drunk and a night with the town prostitutes, who were always very accommodating. But not everyone was in favour, [such as those at the end of the queue- only joking] and for some time there had been continual noise, which often led to fighting in the street. By 1857 it had become unbearable for the inhabitants on the corner of Oxford Street and Willingham Road. The trouble was from the unsightly row of houses on the Willingham Road, known to everyone as 'The Black Horse Row' and a refuge for prostitutes. The prostitutes attracted the troublemakers, and there was often fighting amongst the prostitutes when outsiders tried to muscle in on their business. It came to a head in December 1857, and afterwards business continued more sedately.

In 1854 two Corn Exchanges were considered necessary for improving the trade of the town. Companies of shareholders erected the Market Hall, standing in the market place, and the Corn Exchange situated in Queen Street, each at a cost of about £1,800. However, they did not compete against each other for very long and in 1856 these two rival companies were amalgamated under the title of the Corn Exchange and Market Hall Company limited. Since 1856 the Market Hall was used for the sale of meat, butter, poultry, vegetables and the like, while the Corn Exchange was used for balls, concerts and other functions.

In 1857, Sir A.I. Aston was lord of the manor and the parish contained 1220 acres. Market Rasen was a polling station at the election of members to represent the parts of Lindsey, but very few people in Market Rasen had a parliamentary vote.

The vicarage, valued in King's Book at £10, was now valued at £223 and in the patronage of the Lord Chancellor and incumbency of the Reverend Sanford G. Scobell, who was entitled to the unusual tithe of ale brewed in the parish, and 93 acres 3 roods 17 perches of glebe, mostly allotted in lieu of tithes at the enclosure in 1779. A new organ was purchased for the church, Saint Thomas the Apostle in 1853, at the cost of £150.

The churchyard was closed by an order in council and a new burial ground was bought in 1855. This was two acres on the Legsby Lane on the east side of the town. The land cost £456 and was under the control of a burial board of 9 members. The piece of land on the north side and the chapel were consecrated by the Reverend the Lord Bishop of Lincoln on the 19th February 1855.

After a Royal Commission in 1839 recommended wider police areas, the Police Station was erected by the magistrates for this division of the county in 1849, at a cost of about £2,000. It comprised a commodious courtroom, a lock-up and a house for the superintending constable.

The Court of Requests, established here for this and surrounding parishes under an act passed in 1807, has given place to the county court, held at first monthly at the Police Station, then every alternate month, for the recovery of debts and damages to the amount of £50. The district of this court extended to the 44 parishes of: Bishop Norton, East and West Barkwith, Buslingthorpe, Caenby, Friesthorpe, Faldingworth, Glentham, Hainton, Holton-le-Moor, Beckering, Cold Hanworth, Kingerby, Kirkby-cum-Osgodby, Kirmond-le-Mire, Linwood, Lissington, Legsby, Ludford, Newton-by-Toft, Normanby-by-Spittal, North and South Owersby, Market, Middle, and West Rasen; Stainton-le-Vale, Snitterby, Sixhills, Snarford, Snelland, Saxby, Toft-next-Newton, Tealby, Thornton-le-Moor, East and West Torrington, Usselby, Waddingham, Walesby, North and South Willingham, Wickenby and Wragby.

In 1856 parliament passed the Police Bill and a meeting of the county magistrates was held in Market Rasen to discuss the new

Police Bill. That year J.G.S. Smith of Lincoln was the judge; Thomas Rhodes, clerk; J.U.S. Smith, high bailiff, and Thomas Shearman, bailiff. Petty Sessions being held the first and third Monday in the month.

In 1857 the new County Police Force came into being, and in July of that year Superintendent Charles Forck arrived at Market Rasen to take up his duties.

In 1872 it looked like a take-over by the church, so little or no chance of justice for Mr and Mrs Joe Public, for the magistrates were the Reverend William Waldo Cooper (chairman), the Reverend Julius Henry Rowley, the Reverend Henry Brook Boothby, and Henry Robert Boucherett. George Saffery was clerk to the magistrates. Fighting the church takeover for running the town and people's lives, Mrs Smith, obviously behind the scenes, got the contract … by fair means or foul, for the mail, and the White Hart at Market Rasen, became a centre for the sorting of the post office mail, while letters were still being paid for on delivery. For many years the White Hart was to remain the town and district post office and mail sorting office. It also provided the office of the Lincoln Bank, which issued its own bank notes.

In the mid-1850's the Post Office was still at the White Hart in King Street and Mr. William Goodson junior, was the post-master. Letters arrived from London, Derby, Lincoln and all parts...except the local posts...every morning at twenty-one minutes past six and were despatched every evening at eleven minutes past seven. Letters from the local posts arrived every evening at six and were despatched every morning at a quarter past seven. All due to the enterprise and powers of Mrs Smith, plus a few beers and a shilling or two in the right place.

CHAPTER 9

THE COMING OF THE RAILWAY

Rail Bridge over Queen Street

In the 1650's there were 7 miles of roads in the parish of Market Rasen and they were in very poor state of repair. Most of the time they were flooded and almost impassable. The upkeep of the roads was the responsibility of the surveyors of the highways, and the work was done on contract. But there was very little work done for there were continuous complaints about the state of the roads and walkway. The market place was also continually under fire about its filthy state [that still being said in 1965]. So, in 1659, Sir Arthur Aston, the lord of the manor, put his hand in his pocket and paid £300 for the re-pavement of the market place. He died that same year.

The Turnpike Trustees were also trying to improve the state of roads as the populations increased, and more people travelled. In 1854 the Turnpike Trustees were advertising for contractors to build a bridge, of brick, stone and iron, in the parish of Market Rasen, at what is now the present day Crane Bridge [picture on page 1] near the De Aston Grammar School, on the Turnpike road leading from Market Rasen to Willingham. But, this was a non-starter, for many people wisely avoided the collection points.

The railway started very modestly in 1825 and by 1848, the railway station opened in Market Rasen on the south side of the town. The railway only came to Market Rasen and North Lincolnshire, thanks to the Yarboroughs, who made it known in high places that they wished to have it. It was only by the influence of the Yarboroughs it came; it was they, who brought the railway to Market Rasen and North Lincolnshire.

During planning for the railway, Mr Elliott, an expert from London, said it was not a main line railway line; it was in fact planned as a light railway based on the type then extensively used in Italy. Thus, Market Rasen station opened in 1848 on the Manchester, Sheffield and Lincolnshire branch line between Barnetby and Lincoln. It crosses the main street in Rasen, and Mrs. Cumpstone, wife of one of the town's surgeons, laid the first brick for the bridge on 8 July 1847. The railway bridge was then covered [see photo] to protect shoppers from flying ashes as the trains steamed by.

A railway line was envisaged for this area by the early 1840's and the original plan was for the line to pass about two miles to the west of Market Rasen. The railway killed the plan for a canal to Market Rasen.

Between 1820 and 1830, a survey had been carried out for a canal to be constructed from the Ancholme riverhead to Market Rasen. The plan was that barges from the Humber, would be propelled up to Bishopbridge, and then, taking a left hand turn, travel right through to a new riverhead at church mill, Market Rasen. This would have linked Market Rasen with the Humber, and the Rasen riverhead would have opened up a whole new world. This was a big job, and many from Market Rasen were already engaged on it, one being Towles in Oxford Street.

The railway really took over from the canals. It gave people the chance to travel, and they began to marry people from more distant parts. For Market Rasen the railway changed the face of the town, and it was the death knell for the Turnpike Trust.

Many staff was employed at the railway station and until 1855, Mr.W.B. Taylor was stationmaster. The photograph shows the covered railway station, complete with bookstall, in its heyday. The town was then mighty proud of its station.

The covered in train station at Market Rasen

It was not long before advertising started for 'Cheap Railway Excursions' to the seaside resort of Cleethorpes, and many people from Market Rasen and district, took advantage of the offers. This was one way of stimulating trade to the railways.

Before the coming of the railway, the Ancholme Navigation, which linked the Humber ports to Bishopbridge, had been the main artery for heavy goods into Market Rasen. But from Bishopbridge to Market Rasen, the Turnpike road had two Toll Gates, and this increased the cost of the goods. However, the railway killed the Tollgates at Bishopbridge and Middle Rasen, and not long after the railway arrived, they were abolished.

Many business people were quick to realise the potential of the railway, and with trade flourishing in the town, an outlet could be found for the increased quantities of corn and livestock. They began to satisfy the demand for fresh meat from the industrial midlands. Coal was also big business, and Mr Searby was quick to see the potential with the railway, and he is seen [see photo] with one of his new wagons at Rasen station.

As the railway spread throughout the country, so did the Temperance Movement, and in many parts Temperance Halls were erected, one being at Binbrook. But the strong Rasen Ale, from the three breweries in the town kept them at bay, and local advocates had a hard time to drum-up members.

Mr Searby

Mr Baxter of Market Rasen tried to aid the cause by the formation of a Rechabite Society. The Rechabites refused to participate in agricultural pursuits or drink wine or beer. In a farming community, and a town with three breweries, it was not heard of again. Common sense prevailed. The Temperance Hotel in King Street was the most Market Rasen could offer, and in 1851 Mrs. Frances Hinds ran it. But it did not last long and it was not listed in White's 1856 Directory. Unlike the railway, the Temperance Movement ran-out of steam; but the trains only *just* managed it into the 21st century … and they are running out of puff. So, it is time the breweries returned to Market Rasen, and produce for the 21st century, good old Rasen Ale.... Hallelujah!

CHAPTER 10

THE RICH LAND OWNERS

Waterloo Road

Between 1800 and 1850, the population of Lincolnshire as a whole doubled, but Market Rasen's population actually trebled during this period. The chief innovators at this time were undoubtedly the local lords, who coined in the money, and it is doubtful if they knew or cared where they were really going.

The war with France was still in the minds of many people, for it had impoverished the countryside, and left behind a burden of taxation. Market Rasen had supplied the noble war-horse that lead its master to victory at the Battle of Waterloo, and the town had thrilled to the victories of Trafalgar and Waterloo. To show its elation one of its new streets was called Waterloo Road … today Waterloo Street.

During the period of the war with France the population in rural Lincolnshire increased, and not one in twenty of the labourers could read or write. Many people took advantage of this, including the rich landowners and the religious sections of the community.

The rich landowners refused to build cottages for their workers, for they feared that if cottages were built and formed part of a permanent population, they might become chargeable to, and a burden upon, their estate. They quoted the law of settlement, whereby a man was said to belong to the place where he was born.

Because of this, gang labour was used from Market Rasen on the farms. Many labourers walked many miles to and from work, and their wage was no more than ten shillings a week. They were obliged to work or starve. The poor got poorer. The rejoicing after the victory at Waterloo now seemed overshadowed.

After all Corn Laws were repealed the Duke of Wellington retired from public life after 1845. On 14 September 1852, the *'Old Duke'* as he was called in the 'service' circles, was suddenly taken ill at Walmer castle, his favourite residence, and he passed away peacefully at half-past three in the afternoon. He was laid in state in Chelsea hospital, and then moved to the Horse Guards. It was the last heraldic state funeral in Great Britain.

With the Corn Laws repealed a new system of farming came into being, and this increased production, much to the delight of the landed proprietors. A new world sprung suddenly into being, not unlike the industrial revolution being witnessed in the towns. The Reform Act of 1832 redistributed parliamentary seats to favour growing industrial areas, and by lowering property qualifications, admitted the industrial middle class to the electorate. Charles Tennyson said at a meeting at Market Rasen: *"The Bill is passed."*

As at 1851, Market Rasen was providing 769 people with jobs. Living in the town were 45 agricultural labourers and farm servants. There was also a Rasen cow keeper, a horse dealer, a horse trainer, saddlers, harness makers, four blacksmiths, nine millers and many other trades needed to support a market town. It was a young town with only one person in every 25 being over the age of 65.

The mid-century census showed that the people then living in Market Rasen, fewer than forty-per-cent had actually been born in the parish or its immediate environs. The early 19th century produced the over-all settlement pattern for the town.

By the mid 19th century, all those main people who had received most of the Rasen land at the time of the enclosures had gone. There is no mention in the records of 1850 of Albany Wallis, who had about a third of Rasen's prime land - such an important man, gone without trace. The only Wallis living in Rasen at that date was a certain James Wallis living in Union Street, and he was a joiner by trade. It was most unlikely that he was any relation.

During the early part of the 19th century, Charles Tennyson was building Bayons Manor at Tealby, as he climbed the social ladder. It was to be the last great mansion of major size to be built in Lincolnshire.

It was the time of a new social structure, but it was still much so the 'Upstairs...Downstairs' for Market Rasen, which stood at the crossroads in the downstairs level. But not for Charles Tennyson, who added on the name d'Eyncourt and moved to the top. His father, old George Tennyson of Caistor Road, Market Rasen,who had set up as a solicitor in Rasen around 1774, when he was then aged 24, put himself above the newer profit making class, and ranged himself with the aristocrats. And Charles, his radical son, who as a member of parliament, voted for the Reform Bill, knew which side his bread was buttered, did the same. Around 1820, George Tennyson exploited his position and bought a lot of prime land at Rasen … remember, he was a solicitor and knew what to do to get the best deal … for himself, and moved to Tealby.

The Tennysons never showed an interest in Market Rasen, though they were the second or third largest proprietors in the town, and had very much the best pew in Rasen church up to about 1940. The Tennysons cast the little town aside like an old rag. Old George Tennyson, of Market Rasen, was operating in a much wider field and was, by way of marriage, about the biggest property owner in Grimsby. He was lord of the manor at Glentworth as well as owning property at Caenby, Welton and Tealby.

The 6o-roomed Bayons Manor was completed in 1842, and it had many magnificent apartments filled with valuable paintings and works of art.

Bayons Manor

White's directory said this of Bayons Manor:

The present lord of the manor and owner of most of the soil in Tealby is the Right Hon. Charles Tennyson-d'Eyncourt. FRS, who has erected on the east side of the village an extensive and handsome Gothic mansion in the castellated style. It comprises within its walls some of the lower apartments of the ancient hall in which the Tennysons had long been seated. It is delightfully situated on an acclivity near the fine sheet of water, which is crossed by a wooden bridge in imitation of a drawbridge. The park is stocked with deer.

The country houses of Lincolnshire formed the wealthiest, most vigorous and most powerful grouping to be found anywhere in the country. The local landowners were in control, administratively, as well as judicially, and the landed gentry interpreted for the masses the national constitution under which they lived. The squires pulled the strings and the workers jumped. They were at the top, and working under their say, were the clergy and the parish vestries. At parish level, at county level, and at the top in London, the aristocracy filled every vital function.

At the level of the sessions, or at home in their own parishes, the squires were their own interpreters and men of affairs, directing, controlling and overseeing. Whenever sittings of the quarter sessions were held at Louth, Boucherett seemed nearly always to have presided, with Heneage from Hainton as his vice chairman.

In the first half of the 19th century there were no schools to maintain, and no main roads to keep in repair. Consequently, the landed gentry meeting at the quarter sessions, took the lead in county administrative work, and went beyond their function of merely dealing with offenders.

At the spring quarter session, sat at Louth in 1870 with Boucherett as chairman, and Heneage as vice-chairman, there were 16 squires adjudicating, together with about half-a-dozen clergymen. They might be public leaders, but what could they answer as to public policy and public needs?

Another large estate near Market Rasen was at Hainton Hall, which was owned by the Heneage family. The Heneages seemed to begin by acquiring land, which had belonged to Tupholme Abbey in 1531. In the following year more land was given to Sir Thomas Heneage [as stated in chapter 2] from Sixhills Priory. Sir Thomas Heneage seemed to be in the right place at the right time to exploit the more or less sudden situation, which had arisen in connection with the disposal of monastic properties, in which Lincolnshire as a county, had so many. Sir Thomas, who was a member of King Henry's privy chamber, also acquired a large estate at Grimsby.

The Heneages acquired land for investment, and once they got the land, they held on to it. It was the squire who advised: *"Don't sell land."* The Heneages did not do so.

The squires, having taken the lead in bringing about the enclosures, were now complacent, and Market Rasen, with its little breweries and maltings, got the cold shoulder from them. The land owning families sat back in their huge mansions rather than participating in the changing structure of the countryside. Boucherett from Willingham House stood out as the kindest and most popular personality of his time. Boucherett died about the same time as George Tennyson of Tealby, who at the time of his death had built up an estate of some 6,000 acres.

CHAPTER 11

MARKET RASEN TRADERS IN 1872

Willingham Road

Market Rasen reached its peak in 1871. Its population had increased from 774 in 1801; to 964 in 1811; 1,166 (males 574, females 592, houses 243) in 1821; 1,428 in 1831; 2,022 in 1841; 2,110 in 1851; 2,563 in 1861 and 2,815 in 1871. Its parish contained only 1220 acres.

Market Rasen was thriving and during the previous 25 years many new houses had been added. King Street and Queen Street, the main Louth to Gainsborough Road form one long thoroughfare, with many good shops and several commodious inns. Willingham Road is the main road east. The shop on the corner on the right is Pommie Sands sweet shop. Market Rasen had expanded into a well-built, clean and respectable market town. It had a railway station and parish, head of a county court district, and polling-place for the northern division of the county, in the south division of the wapentake of Walshcroft, parts of Lindsey, Caistor union, rural deanery of Walshcroft, archdeaconry of Stow and diocese of Lincoln.

The trade of the town being chiefly of a retail description, though considerable business was done from the extensive brick and tile yards, three breweries and several malt kilns and corn mills. The inhabitants also derived some advantage from the new spring cattle fair, established in 1854 and held on the fourth Tuesday in Lent. The market, held every Tuesday, was always well supplied with corn and provisions, and on every alternate Tuesday after Palm Sunday, were extensive fortnightly markets for horned cattle, horses and sheep, for which a fair was also held on September 25th. A new fair ground had been provided, near the National School, so that the streets were not crowded with horses, cattle and sheep, on fair days, as formerly.

The little town, snuggled beneath the Wolds, had gone from strength to strength. But had Market Rasen received the backing of one of the rich landowners, during its mushroom period in the early part of the 19th century, it would have developed more, and had a wider role to play. Even without any sort of influential backing, by the early 1870's the town catered for just about every need.
To give one some idea, listed in White's 1872 directory were:

13 schools, 3 of which took boarders; 23 land, insurance, wine, coal, salt and lime agents; 5 attorneys; 4 auctioneers and valuers; 5 bakers and confectioners; 2 banks; 4 blacksmiths; 4 booksellers, binders, printers, stationers and newsagents; 13 boot and shoe makers; 3 brewers; 2 brick and tile makers; 4 bricklayers; 8 butchers; 4 cabinet makers; 3 cattle dealers; 6 chemists and druggists; 2 chimney sweepers; 2 coach and carriage builders; 4 coal

dealers; 5 coal merchants; 7 corn and seed merchants; 6 corn millers; 9 drapers; 3 eating houses; 4 engineers, machinists and agricultural implement makers; 2 fishmongers; 4 gardeners and seedsmen; 2 gas fitters; 2 glass, china dealers; 3 greengrocers; 17 fire and life offices; 16 grocers; 2 hairdressers; 2 horse breakers; 2 horse and gig letters; 3 hosiers, haberdashers; 11 hotels, inns and taverns [see photo of coachman and passengers outside the White Swan Hotel, and the coachman waiting outside the Commercial Hotel and Posting House – now the Gordon Arms Hotel. Both carriages and horses from Mrs Smith of the White Hart Hotel]; 2 beer houses; 4 ironmongers; 8 joiners and builders; 4 land and estate agents; 3 maltsters; 19 milliners and dress makers; 2 music teachers; 1 newspaper [Brigg and Market Rasen Advertiser]; 1 publisher [Market Rasen Weekly Mail]; 5 oilcake merchants; 3 painters and grainers; 3 paperhanging dealers and hangers; 3 photographers; 2 picture frame makers; 3 plumbers and glaziers; 3 provision merchants; 2 register offices [servants]; 3 rope and twine makers; 5 saddlers and harness makers; 16 shopkeepers; 4 stonemasons; 3 straw bonnet makers; 3 surgeons; 12 tailors; 2 timber merchants; 3 tinners and braziers; 4 tobacconists; 2 toy dealers; 2 veterinary surgeons; 6 watchmakers; 4 wheelwrights; 2 whitesmiths [John Woffindin in the Market Place was also bell hanger and gunsmith]; 4 wine and spirit merchants; and 2 wood turners.

What a list. One had no need to go out of Rasen for anything. You could get handmade shoes, suit and hat; plus all your other needs. A fine choice and most were craftsmen at their trades. Quality was first and foremost.

It was the carriers who helped to build up Market Rasen. They were the indispensable link between town and county. The role of the carrier was to convey passengers and goods to and from, place to place, and from the point of personal transport they were slow, and must have been tedious and uncomfortable. But the link between town and village was always a happy, and many times a boisterous one.

The list of Market Rasen carriers at 1872 is quite outstanding. Most carrier services were one-man businesses, and the town based carriers operated from their own homes, while the outside carriers operated from public houses in the town, the Greyhound being the most popular, for Mrs Smith of The White Hart Hotel had her own men and, was the changing place for the stage coaches, so extremely busy.

As stated, the amount of Market Rasen carriers at 1872 was outstanding; and carriers were coming into the town every Tuesday, Wednesday and Saturday mornings, from just about every village within a 12 miles radius; and that included Louth. Captain William Conway Gordon was lord of the manor in 1872, but a great part of the soil belonged to several other freeholders. By this period, the Market Rasen Rifle Volunteer Corps (20th Lincolnshire), formed in 1860, had 90 members. Henry Croft Chambers was the captain; Harry brooks, lieutenant; Samuel Chapman, drill instructor; and Henry Cutting, Quarter Master Sergeant.

The Market Rasen Water Works company was incorporated by act of parliament on 29 June 1875; the water to the town, derived from springs at the foot of Bully Hill, in the parish of Tealby, a distance of 5 ½ miles, is conveyed through iron pipes. No pumping required, as the pressure of the water from the higher level (about 280 feet) forces it to a greater height than any building in the town. The water is soft and pure, and is perfectly fit for use without any filtration. The total cost of the works was about £7,500.

Before mains water, Market Rasen had to make do with water butts, lead pumps, wells and underground storage cisterns. With the need for a lot of water for the malt kilns, one underground cistern was in Serpentine Street, which collected rainwater from the roofs of the malt kilns. A few people had wells and one was discovered during restoration work at the Trustee Savings Bank in the 1980's. Many households had a charcoal filter and in many households, the drinking water was always boiled first. The town pump, standing just beside the town hall, was in constant use as a source of pure water, long before the supply was piped in from Bully Hill.

CHAPTER 12

CHURCHES AND SCHOOLS

The Wesleyan Chapel in Chapel Street

Methodism had been strong in Market Rasen since the early 1800's and between 1747 and 1786, John Wesley had preached at least five times at Tealby. They had a foothold and Methodism continued to grow.

Primitive Methodism crept into the town in 1819, and in 1838 they purchased the former Wesleyan Chapel in Jameson Bridge Street. By 1850 the Methodists began to fallout amongst themselves and they had a serious setback, when the much-needed Wesleyan Day School, opened in 1850, collapsed within three years. This was a hard blow to many people. The continual bickering resulted in a breakaway group being formed, who became the Wesleyan Reformers or the Free Methodist Church [depending on which side of the bed you got out]. This resulted in three Methodist churches in the town.

The large Wesleyan Chapel in Chapel Street was built in 1838, at an expense of £4,500, in lieu of the old chapel in Jameson Bridge Street, which was erected in 1800. The Primitive Methodist chapel in Jameson Bridge Street was rebuilt in 1866 and could hold 300. The Free Methodist chapel in Union Street was built in 1861 and could seat 500. The most imposing building of them all was the Wesleyan Chapel... it commanded a fine position at the bottom of Union Street [see photo]. It was, and still is, the best chapel in Lincolnshire, perhaps even in England.

The vicarage, was now valued at £230 in 1872, and it had been held since 1866 by the Reverend Edwin Cuthbert Harward, M.A., who was entitled to the unusual tithe of ale.

At the western end of the town is the Roman Catholic Church, dedicated to the Holy Rood [see photo]. It was built in 1824 and is an edifice of brick. It was enlarged in 1869 by adding aisles and tower with one bell, at a cost of £2,500, raised by subscription. There are several stained windows, two of which are memorials to Mrs Drakes of Torrington and Reverend Algernon Moore. Adjoining this church is the priest's house, and near to it a school for children.

Market Rasen was well equipped for schools, and there was a continual yearning for knowledge. In the 1850's there were fifteen schoolteachers, four men and eleven women. The main school of this period was the National School for the poor of the parish, and it issued a set of rules for parents and children. For the parents they were instructed to send their children regularly to school, clean, washed and combed, at the appointed hours...before 8.45 am and 1.45 p.m. And, it was made clear that they expected their children to attend Divine Service at the Parish Church, once every Sunday. The rules for the children were very clear: -

1.They must go directly to and from school in an orderly manner.

2.They must pay attention and behave respectfully to their teachers.

3. Look after their books and slates.

4. They must be diligent whilst at school, behave with the greatest reverence during prayers in the school and at church service.

5. They must be kind to one another, and never tell a lie, cheat, pilfer, or swear.

The National School for boys and girls in Willingham Road was founded by the Church of England and built by subscription in 1822, when it was agreed that the master should receive the annuity of £17, bequeathed to this parish for the education of poor children, by Sir George Saint Paule in 1612 and paid by Earl Brownlow.

In the early 1850's there were some private-venture schools for young ladies and young gentlemen, two in King Street, both with two teachers each, at one Walter Browne and Temple Wilmot, and at the other, Misses Annie and Susan Coleman, which they started in 1842, and one in Willingham Street which had three teachers, Misses Ann and Jemima Carr and Miss Martha Darley. The town also had private schools for middle class pupils and these were in George Street, Mary Ann Hooker;
Linwood Road, Ann Harrison; Serpentine Street, Thomas J. Keightly; Waterloo Road, Mrs. Marge Davidson and two in Queen Street, those of Mrs Charlotte Cash and Miss Sarah Browne.

These private schools did offer some form of education, but it is not possible to ascertain the syllabus or the quality of education, for many of them survived only a few years. For many years the inhabitants had campaigned to establish a grammar school in Market Rasen, and this may have speeded-up the closure of the private schools.

Between 1868 and 1869 the National School was enlarged to take 150 children and the average attendance in 1885 was 50 children; John Edward Holmes was headmaster.

The infant's school, built in 1868 for 100 children, had an average attendance of 67 in 1885. Mrs Frances Sussanah Alliss was schoolmistress.

The town also had other major day schools. The Catholics had a large school close to their church in King Street. This could hold 90 children, and in 1885 the average attendance was 40; Miss Lizzie McDonald was the schoolmistress. Little is known about the quality of education the school provided.

The Wesleyan day school, built in 1873 for 240 children, had an average attendance of 139 in 1885; George Henry Howe, master. This was the second attempt by the Wesleyans to contribute towards the education for the town's children. They had started a day school for all denominations in 1850, but it got into financial difficulties, due mainly to the internal fighting of the Wesleyan Reformers, and the school closed in 1853.

In 1885 the private schools in the town were an infant school in Prospect Place, run by Miss Sarah Jane Goldie; a children's day school in George Street run by Mrs Mary Hooker, who was also listed as a corn dealer; Henry Ranyard had a boys school in Queen Street, and the Misses Anne and Elizabeth Rawson, had a ladies boarding and day school in Walesby Road.

One private school that had gone by 1865, was the boarding and day school, kept by the Misses Ann and Jemima Carr, which they had started before 1845. The Miss Carr's school was respectable by all accounts, and they even had boarders from as far a field as London. Now it was gone.

Little is known about the quality of education the schools provided, but seeing that just about all children in Rasen schools could tell the time, read and write, by form one, many before they started school, the town's education of the time was well above that of today.

CHAPTER 13

DE ASTON GRAMMAR SCHOOL

De Aston School - 1863

In 1856 Market Rasen applied for part of the surplus funds of the Mere and Spittal Hospitals to be appropriated to the purposes of education in this small, but healthy and flourishing town. The Hospital of Spittal-in-the-Street is of a very ancient date, and was possessed of property producing about nine hundred pounds per annum in 1872. In the year 1836, the Charity Commissioners, having previously certified the misappropriation of the charity estates to the Attorney General, a new scheme for the better management was issued, after a lapse of 22 years, and enrolled in the Court of Chancery in 1858. The new scheme enacted that the funds, which had accumulated during the period of abeyance, should be appropriated to the erection of a school entitled the De Aston School, after Sir Thomas de Aston, the founder of the charity, and a masters residence, at Market Rasen; which were accordingly built in 1863 [see photo start of chapter – photo below is after extension] from designs by Mr. James Fowler, architect of Louth, at a cost of £5,000 under the -patronage of the Dean and Chapter of Lincoln. The Endowed Grammar School is a handsome Gothic brick building, situated in the midst of eight acres of its own grounds, close to Willingham Road, and had accommodation for 100 boys, 50 of whom are boarders.

De Aston now beginning to grow, note extension on right

In 1885 there were 40 boys, about 16 of who were boarders. The head- master was Rev. Arthur Temperley MA of Sidney Sussex College, Cambridge; the income at that time amounted to £413 yearly, derived from land at Hemswell, left in 1501 by Thomas de Aston. A body of 15 governors managed the school.

It was soon obvious that the new grammar school would be very beneficial to the town. The townspeople had campaigned vigorously for the De Aston Grammar School to be built at Market Rasen, and they had won. It had been a hard fight, for the idea of a grammar school for Market Rasen, was opposed by a number of local aristocrats, one being Sir Charles Anderson. The landed gentry were doubtful about education, and feared it might be against their interest if carried too far. In other words, they wanted to keep the hard working families ignorant. This proves that the landed gentry never wanted to help the town or the people.

Here is an extract from the New Code of 1894: After the 31st August, 1895, the higher grant for Discipline and Organisation, will not be paid to any School, in which provision is not made for instruction in Swedish or other Drill, or suitable Physical Exercises.

The De Aston Grammar School at Market Rasen decided that drill was the best form of physical training for their boys. They said: *"The work of the instructor, once the initial stages are passed, was set for collective drill. By this means, the pupils would gradually obtain a gentle rhythmical movement, to be aimed at as best suited to the growing frames of the scholars."*

To carry out the drill exercises the De Aston Grammar School purchased toy wooden rifles, 42 inches long for juniors, at 6 shillings a dozen; and 48 inches long for seniors, at 10 shillings a dozen. This rifle was specially designed for drill purposes, and was quite harmless. The military gun drill was carried out on land that is now part of the Market Rasen Racecourse. Sometimes the drill was carried out in musical time. From the text book of the period, [it could serve today in the 21st century the only changes being headed 'Urban Survival', and in place of wooden rifles would need to have a Kalashnikov. Just a thought.] So, as I was saying, let us look at the Military Gun Drill for Standards III and IV from that period. Naturally, I have condensed it.

1st Exercise:

Children always take kindly to the gun drill. It is, apart from its youthful conceptions of military valour, inseparably connected with those movements of precision, for which our army is so distinguished; and as this is a quality we gladly like to see in our youthful pupils, the gun drill will be found very useful for the purpose.

The gun used should be a toy wooden one, and harmless in every way. Having handed out the weapons, the pupils must be impressed with an idea of their responsibility and implicit obedience. Silence, smartness, precision, and all other characteristics of a soldier's duty, should be enjoined.

After being arranged, marched on in line, and halted at the word of command, the first attitude to be taught is that of 'Standing at Ease' … then 'Attention' [Fig.1], 'Halt,' 'Salute' [Fig.2], 'Present' [Fig.3] and 'On Guard' [Fig.4], the 'Guards' and 'Attacks'

Attention

Fig. 1

Salute

Fig. 2

Present

Fig. 3

On Guard

Fig. 4

varied according to the discretion of the teacher, and to musical time.

2nd Exercise:

The next command 'On Guard' [Fig.4] is a more important position, and as a good and correct knowledge of it is very desirable, careful attention should be given in acquiring it. Starting, then, from the position of 'Attention,' the left hand should be raised to the barrel, the feet brought to right angles, the left foot leading. Immediately after this position is assumed, the left foot should be advanced about 6 or 8 inches, both knees bent over the feet, the barrel lowered until across the body, pointing upwards and to the left; the butt of the gun should rest against the right thigh, see Fig.4.

3rd Exercise

Right Head Guard — Fig. 5; Left Head Guard — Fig.6; Right Side Guard — Fig.7; Left Side Guard — Fig. 8

The 'Guards' [Fig. 5. 6. 7 and 8] should also be carefully and correctly acquired, not only for the sake of exactitude in position, but also for a means of defence, and this was then shown.

Right Head Attack — Fig. 9; Left Head Attack — Fig. 10; Right Side Attack — Fig. 11; Left Side Attack — Fig. 12

4th Exercise

After the 'Guards' have been properly acquired, the 'Attack' [Fig. 9. 10. 11 and 12] may be undertaken. These were then carried out and perfected and when so, the;

5th Exercise

We will conclude this mimic 'Gun Drill' with one or two pretty finishes. After being re-formed in one line, the whole of the single movements, consisting of 'Stand at ease,' 'Attention,' 'Salute,' 'On Guard,' the 'Guards,' and 'Attacks,' ought to be gone through, varied according to the discretion of the Teacher, and to musical time, a March being best for the purpose. The movements may also be done facing each side, either by the whole line or by alternate members back to back.

Another pretty finish is to 'Form square,' this is done by an arrangement in which a square of double lines is formed: the first line kneel upon the right knee, bringing the gun to the 'Present' position, the lines at the back of them choosing another position, as in Fig. 13.

Fig. 13

After these movements the pupils should be marched back into one line and to the position of 'Attention,' the 'Halt' should be given, and the pupils, carrying their guns upon their shoulders, march off with military precision; in fact, the success of the drill will all depend upon the precision with which it is performed. That was from the Military Gun Drill Text Book for Standards III and IV.

The De Aston Grammar School moved forward gradually through the years and in 1904 new classrooms and dormitories were added, the gymnasium completed and other improvements made, and in 1908 a new laboratory was built for chemistry and physics. The new gymnasium brought about a change in exercises for the boys and there was a gradual rundown of the drill exercises as more and more gym work came into the curriculum.

After the First World War the people of Market Rasen set about their business, and reviewing the position of the De Aston School. Mr P.J. Timms, the headmaster, said at the school speech day in April 1920, that the conclusion had been reached in view of the limited population of the area round Market Rasen, that future growth must necessarily come from an increase in the number of boarders. Before you read Tom Pickering's School days, let us view [see photos] the refectory – the hall used for meals, the dormitory, the Chemical Laboratory and the Sixth Form Room

"The number of 100 boarders could quite easily have been reached," said Mr. Timms, *"if only we had had the accommodation."* Mr Timms went on: *"We now have a sixth form of 13 boys, some of whom are doing special work. I would very much like to establish an advanced course at the school, but at present I*

cannot make an application for one, as I cannot guarantee the required number of boys."

"Not withstanding this limitation imposed by uncertainty, some advanced work was being done, especially in history and mathematics. The ability of the boys to undertake what could often be regarded as quite hard academic work was regarded as the key to the progress, which was being made by the school. The Cadet Corps continued its useful work under Lieutenant B.H. Clews and Lieutenant J. W. Upex, and the school library were serving a most useful educational purpose."

The Refectory

A Dormitory, note the luggage

The chairman of a large gathering of parents was the Very Rev. T.C. Fry, Dean of Lincoln. The Dean said it was pleasing to notice that the school had grown. As a background to this forward movement, which was to be regarded as significant in a little town like Market Rasen, he felt it should be recorded that Lindsey County Council was very anxious to help in the advancement of secondary education, recognising how necessary it was that every boy and girl should have the fullest opportunity for really adequate school training.

The Dean deplored that in the early years of the century, Lindsey had pursued a cheeseparing education policy, and added that they were at that time (1920) inheriting the results of such meanness.

"During the past war," he went on, *"the flower of our youth have laid down their lives for their country. We now have to see to it that we accept our responsibilities towards the new generation, which is coming along. The England of the next generation is now with us here."*

The farming recession had an effect on the De Aston Grammar School, and Mr. Timms, the headmaster, made this clear during an end of school speech in July 1928. *"What is partly holding us back,"* said Mr. Timms, *"is the general depression in industry and the difficulties which are facing our farming friend.*

"The new secondary school at Scunthorpe has also made a difference to the number of our boarders, but the introduction of motor buses into the Market Rasen area is a help where some day boys are concerned.

"There seems to be an idea in the district around that we are full to overflowing but this is not the case. We have vacancies for both boarders and dayboys. May I perhaps add that we attach great importance to the work of giving boys a good grounding in the lower forms."

Presenting the prizes at the 1928 speech day [see early school photo end of chapter] was Mr. S. Mandson Grant, Director of Education for Lindsey and he spoke in detail of what had been done in Lindsey following the passing of the Education Act of 1902. Speaking as an old boy of De Aston Grammar School, Mr. Mandson Grant said: *"We mustn't forget how much has already been done. I myself when I was a small boy here dreamed many things. But it never once occurred to me that some day I might be coming down to see my successors and speaking to them on this important question of*

20th century education policy." On the subject of education expenditure he said, *"Every penny spent on a child's schooling in a great nation like ours is money well spent. What we want to see in our classrooms are the scientists, inventors and technologists of tomorrow who are going to revolutionise the world which is today going forward at a speed which is not falling off as the years pass."*

The Chemical Laboratory

The Sixth Form Room

Mandson Grant mentions the classrooms and scientists, so let us take a look [see photos] at the chemical laboratory and the 6th Form Room. He wanted the educational path broadened with more pupils going on even to the universities. The leaving age for almost all scholars was still 14 even after the passing of the Fisher Act of 1918. But without the director complaining about it, it was a case of Lindsey counting the pennies so far as educational development was concerned.

De Aston Grammar School and Louth were then leading the way in Lindsey. They then had respectively 80 and 90 pupils each. During the mid-1920's one pupil at Market Rasen De Aston Grammar School, was Tom Pickering, who was a boarder, and now recalls his schooldays: *"What I remember most was the food. The food we boarders had was very poor. It was always gooey porridge in a morning for breakfast. Ugh, and for tea time thick doorstep slices of bread and we had our own jam from our lockers. We could have eggs if our parents sent them. I looked forward to the holidays so that I could get a good meal. Every Saturday after the mid-day meal the headmaster handed 6 pence to each boarder. It was then into Market Rasen for sweets and ice cream, but you always had to save a penny for the church on Sunday. Every Sunday we marched smartly to church and we always had to wear gloves and straw boater for church parade. Sunday morning was always letter writing and every Sunday afternoon a walk which was down Legsby Road, through the woods on to Willingham Road and back to the school. The headmaster always went with us. Every morning it was Assembly in the big hall and often singing the De Aston song, which went with a bit of a swing. Every year the headmaster would read to the school, Dickens Christmas Carol before we started our Christmas holiday."*

During that period some of the boarders lived in two wooden huts, about 20 to a hut, and these were sited between the school and Legsby Road. These huts later became the woodwork huts. The Military Gun Drill had now ceased and P.T. (Physical Training) was the order of the day and it was carried out in the gym.

When interviewed in 1984,Tom Pickering was aged 74 and lived at Middle Rasen. When a boarder at De Aston he lived at Hall Farm, Snarford so lived well, hence food a big issue with young Tom. His father and his three brothers had all attended De Aston School. They lived then at Crane Bridge, just across the road from De Aston, so no food problems for them, only young Tom.

The masters who taught young Tom Pickering were P.J. Timms, headmaster, George Timms, headmaster's brother, Court, Clews, 'Ma' Hill, the only woman teacher in the all boys school and she taught French; Guy Smith, Geography and Maths; and Tich Newby. *"All good teachers,"* recalls Tom, *"and you had to watch your step. PT with old Court was very strict. You would all line-up with head and shoulders back."* That was Tom Pickering's School Days. I can vouch for Guy Smith, Tich Newby and Mr Clews, for they all taught me.

The De Aston School continued to make good progress and in 1937 there were 135 boys in the school of whom 64 were boarders. John Timms was still headmaster and there were seven resident assistant masters. The football team was doing better by the day [see photo below]. It was always a good skive for a double lesson.

Top: De Aston playing fields.
Left: De Aston pupils and staff of 1948

CHAPTER 14

THE CHURCH UP TO 1900

The church of Saint Thomas is a building of stone in the early English and decorated styles, consisting of chancel, clerestoried nave, aisles, south porch, organ chamber and vestry, forming a kind of transept, and an embattled western tower with pinnacles containing 8 bells, 2 of which were added in 1867 to commemorate the jubilee of Her Majesty Queen Victoria. Mr. Tom Gibbons, a bell ringer at that time, describes in a pamphlet the arrival of these two bells:

'The ringers formed themselves into a committee, with the consent of the vicar and churchwardens, to raise sufficient funds to procure two lighter bells and so increase the peal to eight. The necessary funds were very shortly raised and Messrs Taylor of Loughborough was consulted and they cast the additional bells. When the bells arrived by train the transport of them from the railway station to the church was made quite a red-letter day. The bells were placed on an open lorry, and preceded by the volunteer band, the ringers walking at each side of them, followed by the vicar and churchwardens. After they were placed in the belfry and ready for ringing they were dedicated by the then Bishop of Lincoln, who

was at Market Rasen on account of a Confirmation, and I had the pleasure of being one of the ringers on that memorable occasion.'

A further quotation from this pamphlet is of interest: *'Christmas Eve the ringers would set the bells going in a peal a few times, and afterwards would take the hand bells and visit various residences. On New Year's Eve, the bells were half muffled, and rung in peal from about 11.30 until shortly before midnight, when just on the stroke of twelve the tenor bell would be tolled 12 times, then the muffles would be removed, and a clear peal or two ushered in the New Year's morning.'*

In the olden days, between the Conquest and the Reformation, the sound of bells filled the air and echoed over the countryside. For each of the many services, a bell summoned the worshippers. The bells peeled for the special blessing of the crops; during haymaking or at the pease-cod or barley, rye, oat or wheat harvest, again to remind the reapers that it is God who giveth the increase. And in times of storm and tempest, the bells would call the people to pray for deliverance for them and their possessions.

The bell rang on Shrove Tuesday, calling all the parishioners of East Rasen to confess their sins and be shriven before Lent. This was later called the Pancake Bell and has sadly now passed into history. The bells of the three Rasens competed with each other, but the church of All Saints at West Rasen was larger and finer than either of the sister churches; and a certain field at West Rasen, called 'Ding Dong' close, was given to the parish in its early days, to ensure the ringing of a bell at night during the winter months.

The interior of the church at Market Rasen was thoroughly restored in 1861, at a cost of upwards of £1,900. On Thursday, 5th June, 1862, the Lincoln Diocesan Society of Architecture held a meeting at Market Rasen, and the secretary, the Reverend Trollope, in speaking of the Church of Saint Thomas said: *"Tower and chancel are all that remain of the old church except some of the lest features of the nave, which has been pulled down, such as the old door-way, the pillars and arches, these having been made use of in the construction of the new nave. The tower possesses a certain amount of solidity that rendered it worthy of retention, and we should have been sorry to lose the transommed belfry lights, which are of an uncommon type. The Sculptured Tablet, representing The Fall of Man, formerly inserted in the southern face of the tower, bears the remains of a legend which is now very difficult to decipher, but was probably a Latin quotation of I Cor. XV.22."*

In White's Directory of Lincolnshire, 1826, there is a notice of this tablet with the following description: Adam and Eve under the branches of a fruit tree on the trunk of which was the dart of death, alluding to the effect of eating the forbidden fruit. But, it fell down and was broken to pieces in 1850.

In the early days the church had a very strong hold on the faith and love of the people; all the daily work and toil and interest, the church hallowed their sorrows and joys. The Tablets on the walls of the parish church each have a story to tell.

The War Memorial Tablet: - This Tablet, which commemorates 72 who fell in the Great War and made the supreme sacrifice for us, their survivors, was erected by public subscription and solemnly dedicated by the Reverend C.S.Nevile, Rector of Wickenby and Rural Dean of West Walshcroft, on Thursday, August 5th, 1920, at 7 p.m., when a large number of the inhabitants of the Parish were present. The inscription reads: *'In grateful remembrance of the above who gallantly gave their lives in the Great War, 1914 - 1919.Their name liveth for evermore.' Ecclus XLIV, 14.*

The vicarage was a poor house, the entrance being from the main street...the coach house and stable were in front abutting on the main street. On Sunday afternoons football was played in the lower part of the churchyard, and it was very popular with the young lads. So popular, it was very difficult to stop.

The present vicarage, a dwelling containing 14 rooms, was built in 1876 when a loan of £1,500 was obtained from Queen Anne's Bounty to be repaid in 30 years. The term was from time to time extended and the last payment was made in 1925. The house is gloomy and badly situated; mainly owing to its proximity to the tower of the church, it is deprived of much sunshine. The vicarage in 1885 had a gross yearly value of £632, including 99 acres of glebe, with residence in the gift of the Lord Chancellor, and held since 1880 by the Reverend Hutchinson Augustus Smith M.A. of Worcester College, Oxford.

CHAPTER 15

PUBLIC HEALTH STANDARDS

Union Street

What was said to be the largest property sale ever held in Market Rasen, took place in the Corn Exchange in 1870, on the occasion of the dispersal of the estate of Mr. John Nash, builder and property owner. About 50 lots in seven parishes came under the hammer on the instructions of the Master of the Rolls in London.

Building was cheap in the 1850's and 1860's, and for around £2000 one could build a whole street like Chapman Street. The speculative builders flourished in Rasen up to 1850. It was easy to take over when they had done the job, and adopt the attitude of the leisured gentleman.

John Nash was a man who had set about building up Market Rasen. He settled in the town about 1820, and with no capital, only his own wits and a will to succeed, he laboured first of all to make bricks. He then built cottages wherever he could get a piece of vacant ground.

When John Nash died he had property in every street and all around the area, and it was said to amount to over £40,000. He was in a way, the founder of the new town of Market Rasen, and it was true to say, that Rasen owed more to lesser known people, who had laboured in their lifetime to advance Rasen, than those who were higher up the social ladder.

Typical lots sold at Market Rasen were:

The residence of Henry Edware Turner, Esq., MD, with gardens extending to the River Rase. Purchased by Mr M.O. Wilson for £830.

Two houses and shops in the occupation of Bean and Co. and Holy Taylor. Purchased by Mr Shepherd, Holton, for £350.

Six houses in Dear Street. Purchased by Mr Gothorp, Linwood, for £360.

The post and telegraph offices with the messuage and shop adjoining in the tenure of George Sharp Young. Purchased by Mr Rhoades for £1,020, who was loudly cheered on making his purchase.

Messuage and shop in the occupation of Mr Bramham Vickers, draper and grocer, and the glass and china warehouse adjoining occupied by Mr George Johnson. Bought in at £810.

The Union Street brewery in the occupation of Mr James Scott. Purchased by Mr Scott for £120.

The Union Street malting offices in the occupation of Mr Joseph Marriott. Sold to Mr Thorpe for £1,000.

Two houses and shops on the west side of Oxford Street. Sold to Mr Coupland for £175.

Four houses on the east side of Oxford Street with the paint shop and ware chamber, the blacksmith's shop and the carpenter's shop. Sold to Mr L.Dawson for £400.

Two houses and shop in Serpentine Street. Sold to Mr Jackson for £255.

Two houses and shop in Serpentine Street, heretofore the Bricklayer's Arms. Sold to Mr R.Glew for £185.

Twelve cottages called the Double Sixes with an area of garden ground. Sold to Mr R.H. Daubney for £300.

Four cottages adjoining each other in Jameson Bridge Street. Sold to Mr.North for £200.

The post wind corn mill on Willingham Road with miller's house and land adjoining. Sold to Mr Hill for £400.

AT TEALBY

The King's Head Inn with gardens and other ground and 2 cottages. Sold to Mr Morrell for £650.

Since 1878. A local board of nine members governed Market Rasen. For the past three hundred years the growing town had been governed by the vestry, a body of persons entrusted with the administration of the temporal affairs of the parish. The parish officers were elected by the towns'men, and the number of meetings held in a year, varied from one a month to every other month, depending upon the work.

Their duties included church affairs, seeing the duties of the church wardens; appointing guardians of the poor, but with the creation of the Caistor Union in 1837, the Caistor Union Board of Guardians took over the care of the poor and the aged; appointing surveyors of the highways and constables, but this latter duty was eased with the building of the Police Station in 1849; and the parish finances, which over the years has always had one problem or another with rate collecting and arrears. In 1885 the area listed was 943 acres, rateable value, £9,515. Lieutenant-Colonel Francis Ingram Conway Gordon was the lord of the manor.

That same period, William Marshall in Waterloo Street, was certainly a very busy man, for he was shopkeeper, rent and tax collector, clerk to burial board and surveyor, inspector of nuisances and collector to local board. Denis Herald, boot and shoemaker in the market place was also the town crier - what an appropriate name for the job.

An advertisement, which appeared in 1885 from the Market Rasen Brewery Company in Oxford Street, offered to supply ales from one shilling per gallon upwards, with free delivery. Joseph Taylor of Queen Street was manager at that time.

During the 1880's there was a marked rise in tobacco consumption, and the Watkinson's were quick to take advantage of it. From their little factory in Serpentine Street they increased their production of clay pipes. They turned out every sort and size to meet the demand. They turned out the cheapest item, namely the clay pipe, to go with cheap smoking material, and it was an irresistible appeal to a vast number of people, and Rasen clay pipes were sold far a field. They must have done very good business, and sold thousands of the clay pipes, for I, as a young lad, found hundreds of pieces of clay pipes in our back garden, what was once part of the brewery.

Some of the small pipes were complete, and because so many, looked as if had been dumped, for all were clean white clay pipes.

By the early 1880's, the Market Rasen Dispensary and cottage Hospital, the former established in 1857, and the latter in 1868, were carried on in one building, that being No.5 Dear Street. Funds for the hospital came from public subscriptions and donations from local prominent people. Money was also provided by the Friendly Societies, which paid sickness benefits, doctor's fees, and funeral expenses in return for weekly contributions. In 1882 Miss Joan Coles was matron, and Mr Herbert Gadd was secretary to the dispensers. They were intended for the relief of the industrious poor; the hospital held six patients, each of whom had to pay a small sum weekly. The yearly average of inpatients was about 20, outpatients 230.

There had been no reports of any serious epidemics of serious disease. There was one death from typhus at Market Rasen in 1859, and typhoid and yellow fever hardly affected the town. These usually occurred from infected water, or brought from abroad. This is one reason why today, in the 21st century, these almost unheard of diseases are returning, and already TB is out of hand in London and the big cities, owing to the influx of immigrants to this once green and pleasant land.

Dr.E.W.Barton, the town's medical officer, warned in 1883 that Market Rasen should be on its guard against a possible cholera out-break. The finger of suspicion was pointed at the local sewage system and at pumps in Waterloo Street, which were close to pigsties. The doctor also said that too many houses were obtaining their water from surface water, which he had found to be unfit for human consumption through contamination. He also said that he strongly suspected that a certain amount of diseased meat was being sold.

Doctor Barton put forward a nine-point plan as a means to help raise public health standards. It is interesting to see how small urban authorities, like Market Rasen, dealt with health standards in Victorian times, and for that reason, let us see what the good doctor advocated. The doctor's nine-point plan was as follows:

1. That the inhabitants should be solicited to drink the water of the Waterworks Company, and to have all water boiled before it is drunk.

2. That river water and well water should not be drunk or used for cooking purposes.

3. That a scavenger should be appointed to remove as soon as possible all animal or vegetable refuse of any kind. All pig sties, stables, ash pits and adjoining places in the town, should be cleansed and disinfected when needful.

4. That no manure heaps or dust or refuse heaps should be allowed to accumulate in the district, and that every care should be taken to remove blood or refuse from the slaughterhouses.

5. That the sewers should be frequently flushed with a view to reducing smells.

6. In certain of the houses stronger action should be taken to reduce overcrowding.

7. That provision should be made for the immediate treatment of diarrhoea occurring among the poorer classes of the community.

8. That proper supervision should be exercised in the markets so that they may be always completely wholesome.

9. That any case of suspected cholera should immediately be reported.

A scavenger is a man employed to clean the streets and cart away the refuse; so, it is obvious that Rasen did not have any at this period, and the good doctor was saying to do so. Now in the 21st century, we have gone full circle, for one does not see any street sweeper.

Post, Money Order & Telegraph Office, Savings Bank & Annuity & Insurance Office, was in the market place with William Cocking the post-master. First mail arrival from all parts at 6.19 a.m., delivery began at 7 a.m. Second arrival from London, Lincoln, Eastern and Southern Counties at 1.30 p.m. with delivery at 1.40 p.m. Box closed at 6.15 p.m. and extra stamp had to be affixed up to 6.30 p.m. The Pillar Letter Box, erected in 1859 in Queen Street; letters collected at 6.10 p.m.; Sundays, collected at 5.45 p.m.

Regular cattle markets began in Market Rasen about 1870, and for the first two or three years, they were held at the top end of the market place. The markets became very well supported, for Rasen was very much at that time a main area for livestock. The Rasen market was ideal for both stockbreeders and butchers, and it had the support of Ayscough Boucherett of Willingham Hall. However, many Rasen people were not in favour of a fat stock market right in the centre of the town. Two small cottages between the Aston Arms and the main entrance to the church had been pulled down, and this area had been paved for the market area. But church people were soon up in arms because the fat stock market was so close to the church, and they thought it was wrong to sell cattle only yards from the church.

With the church taking an active part in the market debate, the 1876 Christmas stock show was held on the fair ground in Willingham Road. But it was not very successful, owing to the fact that it rained and the showground was a sea of mud.

As the number of cattle coming into Market Rasen increased, the argument became more heated, and a town meeting was called to review the situation. The vicar, the Reverend Talbot Hindley, presided over the meeting, and a resolution was passed that a new cattle market centre should be provided, either at the east side of the town, which was the site of the fair ground, or elsewhere, as the lord of the manor Captain William Conway Gordon might decide.

The church people continued to speak out against the cattle market being held so close to the church. *"It is not right that cattle and sheep are penned within yards of the church,"* they said, *"also the cattle pens keep out other traders and in addition to this evil, the stench arising from the excrement of animals penned between the market place and the church, is most objectionable from a sanitary point of view. The newly paved market place is rendered filthy by the presence of so many cattle."*

Throughout this period Market Rasen had the appearance of a Wild West town, with cattle running through the streets. During market days the beer would flow and fights would break out, spilling out into the streets. Drunkenness was a problem that not even the predominantly clerical bench could solve. Market Rasen made its own beer, and liked nothing better than to drink its own beer. The commonest charge on the local court lists was what was called 'drunk and disorderly'.

In 1877, Thomas Nettleship, the local auctioneer, spoke out for the need of larger houses, which would attract families able to spend two or three hundred a year in the town. That same year he sold 1680 square yards of land on the Willingham Road to Mr. John Rawlinson for £98. A similar lot was sold to Mr. A. Padley for £60. Prices per acre were; Willingham Road, £135; Pasture Lane, £82.

Market Rasen had the energy, as its growth had shown over the past few years. But with only its maltings and brick works, the town needed a break that would help it to continue to expand in the right direction. The landed gentry sat on the fence.

Market Place-East Side

Mr. Everett, an official of Mr. Joseph Arch's Agricultural Labourers' League, had his palm well greased, for he was the driving force for the introduction of the co-operation into Market Rasen in 1876. The good people of Rasen did not want them; it received the green light [not from the towns'people] and subscriptions taken. Mr Everett was chosen as secretary, with Mr J Abbott of Middle Rasen, as treasurer. A shop was obtained and business begun. But true to form, corruption and pilfering was rife, and the Market Rasen society went into liquidation, owing the bank a large sum of money while members of the society lost the whole of their capital.

By this time the days of aristocratic rule were coming to an end, as the landed gentry lost control. The rich people living in the large mansions suddenly found out that the goose that laid the golden egg, was egg-bound.

During the 18th century, the ancestral home was all the rage when money was no object. Lincolnshire then became a favourite

place for the mansions, and vast estates for hunting and shooting. But now their days were numbered as the wind of change swept through the countryside, and the landed gentry were feeling the draught.
At the end of the 19th century, Willingham Hall, standing in a well wooded park of 80 acres, the seat of Miss Boucherett, lady of the manor and sole landowner. Mrs. Tennyson d'Eyncourt of Bayons Manor was also lady of the manor and principal landowner.

It was now very clear that no lead or help was forthcoming from the large estates, had it been so, many would not have been alienated in the way they were. What had been needed was a more aggressive approach to farm management, but this was unheard of on the large estates whose function was regarded as being mainly social, rather than productive. Hunting, shooting, fishing, these were what too many of the estates represented. Many people also criticised that clerical gentlemen were monopolising the scene, and were in on everything with the rich landowners. Church of England clergymen were 'gentlemen' one step behind the squires, but now people were saying there were too many of these clerical upstarts; and they were right.

CHAPTER 16

AT THE CROSSROADS

Queen Street

Market Rasen had seen many changes as it approached the end of the 19th century. The town had done well in the first half of the century, but it was not sustained, and without the help of the landed gentry, the growth of the town suddenly ceased. Market Rasen stood on the crossroads and opportunity knocked, and knocked, and knocked. But, those who had the chance to move Rasen away from being dependant on the villages, had not the brains or foresight to do so. Wealth has a creative power and it was not forth coming for the town that never mounted the stairs to the 'Upstairs' position.

The Tennysons had moved right away from the Rasen hierarchy, for to them it was the top or nothing. When the Conway Gordons acquired the lordship of the Rasen manor, they erected a Victorian mansion at Linwood. But the Tennysons wanted the biggest mansion, for to them, money and land meant rank and power. Market Rasen did not offer that, so the Tennyson's had little use for Rasen.

As the end of the century approached, farm wages were around twelve shillings a week. The squires, who were remitting part of their rents, were now made to sit up as agriculture slid into decline. This also hit the farmers who were getting no more than twenty shillings a quarter for their wheat.

A fair number of families kept at least one servant. At the May hiring in 1897 at Market Rasen, there were a large number of girls for hiring. Young girls were engaged at £4 to £7 a year, general servants at £8 to £12, housemaids £12 to £14.

Income tax was at seven pence in the pound. Pepper's stores in Market Rasen market place offered maids' aprons with bibs of full size at 6½ d each.

To give comparison to other wages of 1897, the clerk of the newly formed Market Rasen Urban Council, was paid a salary of £15 a month. The medical officer of health drew 5 guineas a month and a sanitary inspector 13 guineas.

Hamilton Villas

Market Rasen had some nice properties [see photo], which is view from the Willingham Road of Hamilton Villas [later renamed the Woodlands] and owned by my friend Mr Neale who had the furniture shop at the top of the High Street in Lincoln. Today [2003] M.C.Chapman racehorse trainer has the property. With such good properties and nice surroundings, property was much higher in Market Rasen than in any of the Wold villages. In 1892, Thomas Nettleship sold four cottages with gardens at Binbrook for £92 for the four. That same year at Market Rasen, four brick and tiled cottages with outbuildings and gardens, Nos. 11, 12, 13 and 14 Linwood Road [see photo that was taken just after the sale of the four properties. Note the pride in the clean steps. From Italy, when my friend Mike Fletcher was mayor, I sent to him and told him to buy one of the Linwood Road terrace houses and preserve as a 'time warp' of that period. Never did do.], was sold to Mr. William Beech for £300. Six brick and tiled cottages with outbuildings and gardens, known as Waterloo Terrace, which had been built in 1848, was withdrawn at £400. A farm on the Caistor Road, with dwelling house, farm buildings and 40 acres of arable and pastureland was passed at £700.

Linwood Road

The reins of control were passing into new hands, and under the provisions of the Local Government Act of 1894 the town became governed by an Urban District Council of 12 members, having from 1878 been under the control of a Local Board. The Urban District Council started with an office of sorts in Mill Street and board day, first Wednesday in the month at 10.30 a.m. Parish clerk was George Shaw, market place. The parish contained 974 acres; rateable value £9,434. Lieutenant-Colonel Francis Ingram Conway-Gordon, of Lynwode Manor was still lord of the manor and principal landowner. Rasen still had a town crier, a certain George

Castle, of 23, Jameson Bridge Street, who was also billposter for the town.

The County Police was made up of 21 divisions, Market Rasen being one division at inspector level. It served stations at Binbrook, Faldingworth, Market Rasen, Middle Rasen, Osgodby and Tealby. Melbourn Holmes was inspector, with one sergeant and seven constables.

The Market Rasen Weekly Mail and Lincolnshire Advertiser were established in 1856, and published on Saturdays, by Thomas H. Whittingham, the proprietor. The Mail soon became known as the tablecloth paper, for in many poor houses in the area, people used the newspaper as a cloth for the table. The newspaper opened out into one large sheet of paper and would just cover the table. At the end of the century, the Market Rasen Mail was still going strong and reporting all the news. The paper cost one penny.

The Post, M.O. & T.O., T.M.O., Express Delivery, Parcel Post, Savings Bank and Annuity & Insurance Office had moved from the market place to No.7 Queen Street and William Cocking was still the postmaster. A note in the postal records in 1897 states: 'Market Rasen - Cocking W, Postmaster above 60. Not to be retired.' But that was to be short lived, for in 1901 there was a note saying, 'Inefficient through age - Retirement.' Mr Cocking appealed against retirement, but was overruled. Miss C. **A.** Cocking was appointed postmistress, and she was to remain as such until 1922.

The New Post Office in Market Rasen opened in 1894, and business was good and rural post extended. Nevertheless, within four years the office was downgraded from Class D to Class E.

Market Rasen had a good postal service with first arrival from all parts at 6.10 a.m.; delivery starting at 7 a.m.; second arrival, 1.34 p.m. from all parts; delivery starting at 1.50 p.m.; third arrival, 7.15 p.m.; delivery starting at 7.30 p.m.; mail dispatched, 8.25 and 10.40 a.m. and 6.30 p.m.; Sundays, 6 p.m. Letters could be now posted at the railway station, with extra stamp, between the arrival and departure of the train timed to leave at 7.15 p.m. The Pillar Letter Box in Queen street was cleared at 10.30 a.m. and 6.20 p.m.; Sundays 5.45 p.m. The Wall Letter Box in Willingham Road, cleared at 5.55 p.m.; Sundays, 5.40 pm.

By the year 1900, William Marshall from Waterloo Street, who only a decade earlier had been a man of many different hats, had gone. There was a William Marshall listed as a farmer at 62,

Willingham Road. But, it is not possible to say if it is the same William Marshall.

James Cooper, 2 Mill Street, was now surveyor, sanitary inspector & collector. The post of inspector of nuisances appointed under the 'Nuisance Removal Act for England 1855', had gone. The new Council must have decided that Market Rasen no longer had any nuisances!

A new post listed, was carried out by Charles Schrimshaw of 2 Dear Street, and it was as, castrator. Whether this was to carry out the sentence of the court, or for the animals, it does not say! If it were for the former it would be wise to bring back the post today.

Eleanor May's School Days

Visible changes had been made in the schools at Rasen by the turn of the century. The Elementary Education Act of 1870 was Great Britain's first comprehensive act for establishing tactical supported, free elementary schools nationwide, as well as a system of educational supervision through local school boards. Free education meant the elimination of all school pence, payable by parents. The broadening base of education meant the town was entering an entirely new era. My mother, Eleanor May, attended a private school that became Sheffield Manor School, the forerunner of Miss Gledhill's School in Rasen, and seen here [see photo] with group of children of the private school. Eleanor May is second girl from right, back row.

The De Aston Endowed Grammar School at Market Rasen, had at this time, 40 boys of whom 18 were boarders. The Rev. Arthur Temperley was still the headmaster. The school's income was still the same. De Aston School was advertising that it had vacancies for boy pupils under 13 at £1- 13s - 4d a term.

The National school in Willingham Road (boys) had an average attendance of 65, George Evison, master; the girls' school had an average attendance of 66, Miss Isabella Bell, mistress. The infants still had Mrs. Frances Susanna Allis as mistress, and their average attendance was 75. The Wesleyan mixed school, had an average attendance of 135. George Howe was still master, but he had been joined by Mrs. Emma Higgins, mistress.

The managers of the Wesleyan day school, had now come into line, and decided to comply with the requirements of the new Elementary Education Act, though the adoption of the act meant a loss to the management as the average annual fee was in excess of the government fee grant, of ten shillings per child. The parents, who believed that their children were receiving a higher standard of teaching, readily paid higher fees. Income received by the Market Rasen Wesleyan school during the year 1897 was £212- 8s- 10d. Included in this sum a government grant of £117- 5s- 6d and there was also a fee grant of £45- 10s; and a drawing grant of £4- 5s- 6d. Scholars pence brought in £2- 7s- 6d and there was a general amount, including rent, collections and subscriptions of £43- 0s- 4d. The school paid out £178- 0s- 6d in salaries, and £28- 6s- 2d for lighting, fuel, stationery and cleaning. Special sermons were preached at the Wesleyan Chapel as a means of raising funds.

The Catholic school in King Street had now closed, and from the other smaller private schools, Jane Goldie, Mary Hooker, Henry Ranyard had gone. Only Miss Elizabeth Rawson's, boarding and day school in Walesby Road remained at this time.

The Fire Brigade was formed in 1872, but for years previously there was a fire engine in the town but according to the records, not in much of a state to fight fires. In 1882 Mr J. Boyers was superintendent, and since 1869 the fire engine was in Kilnwell Road, in a well-built shed for that purpose. By 1900, Charles Drayton was captain, with one engineer and six men.

Around 1890, my grandfather, Charlie Hall, founded the Market Rasen Town Band [see photo – he is on the left]. The photograph was taken in 1906. The town has always been keen in sports [football in the churchyard] and during this period the Market Rasen Cricket Club was active. It was established in 1816 as the Thursday Cricket Club [see photo which was taken in 1910] and played under the rules of the Marlebone Club that formed 1787.

Market Rasen Town Band

Thursday Cricket Club

The Market Rasen Dispensary & Cottage Hospital was still in Dear Street, attendance daily (except Sunday) from 9 to 11 a.m.; Tuesday 11 to 1 p.m. George Henry Barton and Oscar Bagster

Trumper, physicians and surgeons at 34 King Street, Market Rasen, and John Crisp Griffiths, physician and surgeon and medical officer and public vaccinator Tealby No.8 district, Caistor union, were the medical officers. Arthur Augustus Padley, from Walesby Road was the treasurer; Wallis Byron Jevons, Hon. Sec; Henry Brice, dispenser. Mrs. Edna Casswell was matron.

In 1885 there were three bank agencies and two breweries in Market Rasen. By 1900 there were only two bank agencies and one brewery. The brewery that survived was the Market Rasen Brewery Company Limited with its offices and its brewery in Oxford Street. At that time it advertised ales and stout from 8d per gallon and upwards. Guaranteed brewed from the choicest Kent hops and English malt only. William Pilgrim who lived at 11 Chapel Street was manager. The first manager at the Market Rasen Brewery was Mr Taylor, and both Taylor and Pilgrim had their names on all the bottles. After Pilgrim left, Mr Tillett took over but by now the Brewery had stopped putting the name on the bottles, and in place they put a star, which became known as the Rasen Star.

Joseph Marriott was still apparently successful with his maltings in Oxford Street. Also, the Brick and Tile Company showed no sign of production falling off at their works up Willingham Road. But others had different ideas about the prosperity, and more people from the Rasen district were immigrating to Canada, than ever before. Emigration had been going on for many years, and this had a deepening effect on many Wold villages. As the housing position worsened, coupled with the decline in farming, many people decided to emigrate. Farm wages were very low and many people worked all day for a shilling, some even for six-pence.

However, Market Rasen was much better off than the Wold villages, and many other market towns. The local squires were in control of every aspect of rural life and they pulled all the strings. They paid little or no taxation, and yet they owned thousands upon thousands of acres. The Tennyson-d'Eyncourt family at Bayon's Manor and other local squires were sitting pretty upon their vast estates. At Rasen, though it was never firmly under the control of any single squire, you could still see the people jump when they pulled the strings. They were in control of the whole establishment.

It was Disraeli who said that England was in danger of becoming two nations, namely, those who had all the privileges, and those who had none. The people of Market Rasen were well aware of the overriding position of the landed gentry of the great estates lying all around them. However, by the turn of the century there was a strong new middle class in Market Rasen.

At the turn of the century May Pole dancing was very popular, and there was always plenty of interest going on. Market Rasen used to be visited by the original Wombwell menagerie. The markets played a very important part of the town's economy. After looking round the market, people would go for lunch at an Eating House in the market place or in King Street, or a beer at the Hotels, Inns or Taverns. People supported the local shops, which supplied a wide variety of top quality goods.

The Halpenny Family supported the town's trades people, and Eleanor May only wore bespoke shoes and boots, and these can be seen [see photo] her boots, which she loved, for so soft. These handmade in the town and seen here with her sister Sue.

The variety of shops is a much uncommon sight now. Frederick Dunn of 35 Queen Street always had a wonderful selection of boots and shoes, at a price to suit everyone. Tradesmen in those days were experts in drawing the crowds and children loved it. One such Rasen character was Tommie Bonnett, furniture dealer and butcher, 20 and 21 Willingham Road, and butcher, Queen Street. To get your attention Tom would break up odd items of furniture. Warren's merry-go-rounds was always well patronised at the fairs, as were Pea Joe's shrimps and oysters, and Hall's gingerbreads.

A steeplechase meeting was held here annually early in the spring, and a horse and dog show on the first Wednesday after the 25th September. By 1900 Thomas Ellrington Smith of 2 Jameson Bridge street, was veterinary surgeon and secretary to the Market Rasen Horse and Dog Show. William Frearson was honorary secretary to the Market Rasen Union Hunt Steeplechases, King Street. Others were: Market Rasen Angling Association, 1, King Street, with A.J. Tillett, honorary secretary; Market Rasen Choral Society in Queen Street, Henry Payne, hon. sec; Market Rasen and

District Cricket Club, C. Hinds, hon. sec; Joseph Hackney was secretary of the Market Rasen Quoits Club and the Market Rasen Pig Club, Mill Street.

The Market Place-Looking North

At the turn of the century, the places of worship in Market Rasen were St. Thomas's; Holy Rood Catholic Church; Free Methodist, Union Street; Primitive Methodist, Jameson Bridge Street; Wesleyan, Chapel Street; and the Salvation Army, Willingham Road.

Nearly everyone went to chapel, and the Methodists proved more than any other section of the community, how a family could combine chapel going, and be happy in their work. Methodist families managed to build up really good businesses, and what they promoted, because of their belief in the virtues of hard work, was economic growth. As traders, the Methodists were one up on the church people.

Market Rasen had been brought up on religion and Rasen children on Bible stories. In Whittingham's bookshop, there were shelves upon shelves of religious books, at least six different kinds of Bibles, the Methodist hymnbook and the Church hymnal.

CHAPTER 17

INTO THE 20th CENTURY

Market Place-South Side

Market Rasen into the 20th century and the town moves forward into a new era. The shops on the south side of the market place [see photo] move forward with quality goods and service. The large building at the end on the left is the White Hart Hotel; just before it, the Greyhound.

In 1902 the flags were out at Market Rasen to celebrate the ending of the Boer War. Everyone turned out in the market place in their Sunday best. The town band played military tunes. The Boer War, also known as the South African War, was fought between Great Britain and the two Boer Republics - the South African Republic (Transvaal) and the Orange Free State - between October 1899 and May 1902. The total British military strength in South Africa reached nearly 500,000 men, whereas the Boers could muster no more than about 80,000.

At first the British had many losses, and the Boers beat the British in a number of major engagements, and besieged the key towns of Ladysmith, Mafeking, and Kimberley. The British were fighting in a hostile country over difficult terrain, with long lines of communications, while the Boers, mainly on the defensive, were able to use modern rifle fire to good effect, at a time when attacking forces had no means of overcoming it.

Kitchener responded with barbed wire and blockhouses along the railways, but these failed, and he then retaliated with a scorched-earth policy. Over 20,000 died in the carelessly run concentration camps. But Kitchener's drastic and brutal methods slowly paid off and the tide turned.

During the early part of the 20th century, the workingman in Market Rasen was earning £1 a week. At this period the town hadn't a single council house. The eating habits had changed and this meant a change in shopping habits, which in turn had a marked effect on the little shops of the town. When the new middle class emerged, so did the five-course meal, soup, fish, meat, dessert and savoury.

In 1902 Mr. Mawer offered the Railway Hotel for sale. It was described as one of the most important licensed houses in Market Rasen. With the hotel was stabling for 40 horses and capacious warehouses. The hotel accommodation comprised a bar parlour, a liquor bar, a commercial room, 8 bedrooms, 2 kitchens, a tap room, a dairy, cellar, boot house, yard and a carriage house. The Market Rasen Brewery Company bought the Railway Hotel for £2,370.

De Aston Grammar School football team-1907

Between 1900 to 1910 the De Aston Grammar School was considered to be doing very well, compared to other schools of its type. The football team [see photo] photographed in 1907, looks good and strong. The first player on the left of the back row – as looking at picture – is Stanley Hird, whose father, John Robert Hird, was manager of Midland Bank [now HSBC] in the 1920's. It was one of the leading grammar schools in Lindsey. There were 100 to 110 boys at the De Aston School of whom half were boarders.

The good people of Market Rasen warily received Balfour's Education Act of 1902. They thought that the new act was slanted in favour of the church schools, and this produced a split in educational thinking at Market Rasen.

There were more chapel people than church people in the town, and what the chapel people didn't like, was that the church schools were now to be supported by the rates. There was also to be closer integration with the grammar schools. The chapel people wanted to know why they should be bound to send their children to church schools, when they disagreed with their religious teaching.

Market Rasen had been built up on chapel going. Mother stayed at home to cook the Sunday dinner, while the rest of the family went to chapel. Even as late as 1900, Market Rasen was the central point of a circuit containing 27 Wesleyan chapels, 53 local preachers, an evangelist, and 15 local preachers, who could be drawn upon in other neighbouring circuits.

The new middle class structure had grown up in the town, accompanied by the strength of the chapels. At working class level there were also differences in the social scale. Outside of the town, the traditional class structure, that of the aristocracy, the middlemen (tenant farmers) and the working class, still continued.

Thomas Nettleship, who had been the first chairman of the new urban council, died in 1905. He had been a staunch Liberal, and had made out that he had been in favour of the scheme for the town to take over the Town Hall and the corn exchange. If Nettleship had been serious for the town to have the buildings, he could have done what Arthur Cocking did … bought them, then sold them to the town at the price he paid for them. But did he? No, did he hell. It was Thomas Nettleship who first gave the name of the Town Hall to the building, his building. Nettleship had two offices at the time, one on either side of the main entrance. With a change of use for the building he thought that to have the postal address of 'Nettleship,

Town Hall, Market Rasen,' was the best possible, and I must agree, it was.

During a visit to Market Rasen in 1906, Sir Robert Perks, MP, attacked the closeness of the link-up, which was found in this area, between the Anglican Church and all the voluntary schools. Perks stated: *"It is high time that our local schools should remain true to their primary purpose of teaching, and less of a nursery for the Established Church."* Perks did his electioneering round Rasen in a carriage and pair. His carriage stood at the bottom end of Union Street, while Sir Robert went from house to house conversing with the town's people.

At that time, Liberalism and nonconformity, showed up very clearly in Market Rasen, and Perks was preaching to the converted. After the Liberal landslide of 1906 the aristocracy were pushed back a few paces, and it provided the prudent Nonconformists among Market Rasen traders with a real boost. The Liberal victory also put the wind in the sales of Sir Robert Perks, who announced in the commons that there were more nonconformists sitting in the House than there had been since the days of Cromwell. Sir Robert was the originator of the Million Guineas Fund, which resulted in the Central Hall at Westminster being built by the Wesleyans.

Eleanor May's mother and father with the first pony and trap [Governess car] in the town.

At Market Rasen, the Liberals were flushed with their success and a new Liberal club opened, and hailed as one of Rasen's major buildings. Lloyd George put up the income tax from a shilling to 1s- 2d in the £, the defeated conservatives denouncing it as an outrage. Also, there was a special tax on petrol, Perks, the local Liberal MP, said that motor cars were a luxury toy for the rich. In Rasen at that time, the only means of transport for both rich and poor was pony and cart, not all flush like Sir Robert. Eleanor May's mother and father [see photo] had the first pony and trap [Governess car] in the town. The picture shown was taken in 1901 at the bottom of Mill Road. The Modern School was later to be built on the land at the back. In the photo – left to right – Mrs Hall, daughter Eleanor May [later to be Mrs Harvey Halpenny], Mr Hall, businessman of the town with shop at 54 Queen Street, and daughter Sue [later to be Mrs Egan and live in Oxford Street].

Motorcars would have made it easier for the town's people and traders in Market Rasen, for through the summer months dust was a major problem. In 1911 the council decided to put into practice, a new scheme for the watering of the roads throughout the summer months. Dust blown up by the wind and fast stepping horses, was one of Rasen's greatest problems. The dust on the road was composed chiefly of dried horse manure, and this dust settled in the butcher's shops.

In July 1912 a report was made to Market Rasen Urban Council, that children of the town were playing cricket in the street, and were running with wheelbarrows on the footpaths. They were being a nuisance it was said, and Mr. Padley, the clerk, said that in a matter like this, either the police or the council's surveyor could take action. In defence, Mr. Benjamin Hardy was the only one with any sense, for he pointed-out that the children had nothing to do and nowhere to go. Rasen's crying need, he declared, was a recreation ground. Mr. Cooper thought that some of the children's trucks were actually being used as perambulators. Tommie Bonnett seized on this remark, and said it might actually help him, because he had some perambulator wheels, which he would be pleased to sell. Like the ostrich with its head in the ground, the council decided to 'take note' of the position, and to express the hope that in the longer term a recreation ground might be afforded.

The wheels of improvement moved very slowly in Market Rasen, the town had to feel its own way, and it is sad to note that in

1913, there were thirty or more vagrants calling each week at the Market Rasen vagrant wards in Chapman Street. Also, there had been a steady rise in people begging for food, and two men were caught in George Street in the same day. Wages were still very low, and Market Rasen had very little work to offer. Also, there was no unemployment pay and little in the form of pensions. The 1911 census showed there were 609 inhabited houses, and 33 un-inhabited houses in Market Rasen. The total population was 2296. The urban council meetings, were held on the first Wednesday in each month at 10.30 a.m. in the boardroom at the old Corn Exchange.

At the May hiring fair at Rasen in 1913, there was still a demand for domestic servants; Cooks £18 to £20 per annum; general duties £9 to £16 per annum; housemaids £10 to £16 per annum; between maids £10; kitchen maids £10 to £14; house parlour maids £16 to £18 per annum and young girls first into service £4 to £5 per annum. Good ploughboys could get £14 to £16 per annum, plus their keep at the farmhouse.

It was the custom in Lincolnshire to engage young men for farm work, and girls for domestic service on a yearly basis. It was a verbal contract, and when a servant had made a bargain, with his (or her) potential employer, the latter would give a coin to the servant. This was called a fastening penny.

The year's service ended on May 14 in Lincolnshire, and this was known as 'pag rag day'. The staff received their year's wages on that day, and then had a week's holiday, after which, they either returned or went to the May Week hiring for other work and place, and the whole cycle of events was repeated. To be in 'service' was the main form of employment.

During this period the war clouds were gathering over Europe yet Lord and Lady Heneage from Hainton Hall, spent part of the winter in Germany. The landed gentry with their great estates were still in force and living in the land of milk and honey, which did not include Market Rasen.

But, the wind of change was blowing, and it was to affect everyone, even the landed gentry and the church. The gap between the church and the chapel was still as wide as ever. The Church of England represented the established order, which was the ruling power [the Chiefs] in Lincolnshire, while the chapels represented the ordinary people [the Indians].

A few months before the outbreak of the First World War, cinematograph pictures started at the Town Hall on Tuesday and Thursday of each week, and they were very well received by the people of Market Rasen. The cinema opened up a whole new world, and Charlie Chaplin became a household name, as he played out his antics on the silver screen accompanied by suitable piano music. View of King Street [see photo] shows on the right the Town Hall Cinema … where I spent many a night.

View of King Street. Note the gaslights

During this period there was a growing suspicion with Germany, and this was very much so in Market Rasen. However, one family which didn't seem to join in this hostility, were the Alingtons of Swinhope House, Swinhope, near Binbrook. Admiral Alington, speaking on a public occasion at Market Rasen, said it was a great mistake to think of the navy as just having a protective role in the North Sea. He was in favour in providing a presence on the seas of the world. He maintained that once we set aside our desire to preserve the freedom of the seas, then it would follow that our standing as a major power would be imperilled. He spoke of discussions, which he had had on this subject with the Kaiser and his brother Prince Henry. Admiral Alington said: *"I found that both the Emperor himself and also his brother, Prince Henry, were ardent in their professions of friendship to this country."* But, the age of peace, represented by Admiral Alington, were now drawing to an end. He was in cloud cuckoo land.

CHAPTER 18

FIRST WORLD WAR AND HORSES

Lincolnshire spindle-sided wagon

Right up until the First World War the horse was still the main form of transport for farm produce and for most work on the land, and the main wagon was the Lincolnshire spindle-sided wagon [see photo above]. Normally single-shafted with a gear horse in front. The above photograph shows gear horse in front of a pair. The wagon is the property of Robert William of North Owersby. Most of the implements were horse drawn, and two good horses would plough an acre a day. In different parts of Lincolnshire different methods were used. On the Lincolnshire Wolds, four horses, all abreast to an implement was the method, whereas, in the Lincolnshire Fens, four horses still used, but yoked two before two, and a man would walk between the first pair, while a second man walked behind guiding the second and also the implement.

Three horses would drill 15 or 16 acres of corn a day. Drilling corn was a very tiring job. One horse was yoked in the shafts and two yoked in front. A youth would walk between the first pair and another man led the shaft horse with a leading-stick attached to the horse's bit. The object was to guide horse and drill so that no piece of land was missed and none drilled twice over, which in Lincolnshire terms was called 'Wide Wheelings'. There was an art in this, only acquired by practice. A third man would follow behind the drill keeping an eye on the flow of seed. His job was also to lift up the colters [a cutting knife fixed to the front of a plough-beam to cut the grass ahead of the ploughshare], while the drill was turned round at each end of the field, and to re-fill the seed box.

Another job that needed skill and a lot of energy was ridging potatoes, and it was done with a single furrow plough. The plough was without wheels, therefore the depth and width had to be controlled by the man holding the plough handles. Normal practice for ridging potatoes was to set out the field in 'lands' 30 yards wide, and to operate round and round.

A three-horse team for the two furrows plough

Ploughing was easier, but it meant for the ploughman, walking ten or more miles a day, besides feeding the horses night and day. Most of the ploughing in the Market Rasen area was done with two horses, side by side, but with two furrows plough [see photo] needed a three-horse team. Many times a fresh pair of horses would change over at midday.

To plough or drag difficult fields, a pair of steam ploughing engines (steam cultivators) would be used. The cultivators were engaged on a 'piece work' basis. One engine was either side of the field with a steel rope attached to the plough, or cultivator, which was pulled across the field by one or the other of the engines. A man sat on the implement to steer as it was pulled backwards and forwards on the steel rope, which was fastened to a large revolving drum under each engine.

A sail reaper in action

A wagoner was engaged all day to supply coal and water to the two steam engines. The two engine drivers and the ploughman had a van in which they lived.

At harvest time the corn was cut with a sail reaper [see photo], which was drawn by two horses. Sails swept the corn off a table and then left it in handy heaps ready to be tied into sheaves, and stooked by hand.

A shock was a pile of sixteen sheaves. The women and children usually tied the sheaves. This task was replaced by the introduction of the binder, which made and tied the sheaves mechanically.

All the sheaves were led to a stack by horses, and building the stack from the sheaves was a great art. The stacks were thatched so as to keep the corn dry.

Threshing corn was another job, which called for a lot of energy. The first threshing machines were moved by horses, as were the portable steam engines.

Threshing machine at work

Eventually, the machines moved on the road under their own power. The threshing machine [see photo that shows one at work] was driven by a steam engine. During threshing a wagoner would be engaged to lead water to the steam engine. He would also carry the corn from the threshing machine to the barn. The sacks of corn weighed 18 stone for wheat, 16 stone for barley, and 12 stone for oats. Many men carried over 150 bags in a day.

On Mr Willey's farm

A wagoner would feed and attend to four or six horses. Wagoners were very experienced horsemen, and a good man gave his horses every care and attention. They had their own special recipe for horse powders, to keep their team on top form. Each horse was allowed a stone of corn a day, but for a shire horse working regularly, it needed a little more. On Mr Willey's farm near Market Rasen [see photo] we see Mr Willey and family leading corn at harvest time in 1904. I think his pretty daughters are there just for the camera, and they certainly add beauty.

Horses and wagons rolled into Market Rasen with farm produce, either for the mills or the railway station, their load being twenty quarters of corn. To get to Market Rasen, many teams needed an early start, and this meant that the wagoners had to be up early. The horses needed at least two hours feeding time every morning before 'yoking' out to work.

Before I mention the combustion engine, let me mention briefly, how horses were used in Canada for providing power. My father, a great horseman, he once rode all through the night to get the doctor for his mother – he was ten years old. However, I digress. Before the popularity of the petrol engine, what was called 'horsepower' [see photo below] was used on Canadian farms when my father was a young lad. The operator can control the speed of the movable treadmill on which the horses walk constantly uphill providing the power. In the remote areas there were smaller models for dogs used for churning milk into butter and so on. In the photograph you see the power being used to saw logs. Now back to Lincolnshire.

The internal combustion engine brought great changes in the county, and the carrier and his horse died a natural death. Transport became quicker, for time was money. Tractors started to appear on the farms around Market Rasen during the First World War but it was to be many years, before they took over completely from the faithful horse. In the photograph we see them leading corn by steam lorry [see photo] but it was soon to be superseded.

The early tractors were not easy to handle, and in many cases they needed a second man to work the plough. Therefore, in the early days, the horse could compete very favourably with the mechanical beast. The horse was well rooted on the farm and it was self-sufficient. During the 1914-18 war, the annual cost of keeping a heavy horse was estimated at £27. The break down for this was £17 for feeding and £10 to cover blacksmith and veterinary costs.

Steam work on the land

At the outbreak of the First World War the warhorses played a major part. They were needed in vast numbers, to give some idea, an infantry brigade of four battalions (about four-thousand men) needed in the field over two hundred and fifty horses and mules. Cavalry, artillery and supply services all needed horses. Losses were very heavy, and of more than a million war-horses, bought by the British government up to May 1917, one in four died. 143,000 died in France alone. Market Rasen supplied many of the warhorses, for Lincolnshire has long been famous for a fine breed of horse, and at Horncastle during a week in August, one of the greatest horse fairs in England was held for many years. Lord Yarborough's estate would always send over 50 horses that had been used for hunting, to the sale.

The bond between man and horse was great, and one of the most human pictures of the First World War, was a British soldier on the battlefield, holding up the head of his dying horse and saying *"Good-bye, old pal!"* was it a Market Rasen horse?

Market Rasen was not in the front line during the 1914-18 war, and the nearest airfields were South Carlton and Scampton, for most early bomber stations were built on the steep Lincoln Cliff. The Humber was a good entry point for the Zeppelins, and not long after the outbreak of the war, a Zeppelin was in the area of Market Rasen, possibly after the airfields at Lincoln or Gainsborough, but more likely it was lost, and an odd bomb or two dropped a few miles away from the town. The bombs prompted Market Rasen into action, and after a hurried council meeting, Mr. Page was told to stop the town clock from striking. The council, in its almighty wisdom, had come to the conclusion, that if the navigator of an enemy aircraft heard the town clock striking below, he would be able to pinpoint the position of the town. [Rumour had it beans were also withdrawn] The striking mechanism wasn't wound up any more, and the clock remained silent for the duration of the war.

In the autumn of 1914, Tommie Bonnett, on his own initiative, sent a note of praise to the French President, Monsieur Poincaire. Back came a reply addressed to *"Monsieur le Maire de la ville de Market Rasen."*

Eleanor May Hall and her sister at a munitions factory

Market Rasen saw many changes during the war, and the town was packed with soldiers and horses. Many people left the town to work in munitions factories as part of their war effort. One such person was Eleanor May Hall, of 54 Queen Street, Hall's greengrocery. While on war work [see photo – Eleanor May bottom left, her sister Sue next to her], Eleanor May Hall met and later married Harvey Ashton Halpenny, a Canadian soldier who had been sent to hospital in England. He was lucky, for he was classed as 'walking wounded', and had to stand, leaning on two or more other 'walking wounded', for hours on end, for the beach in France was packed full of wounded men.

Mud and blood that is what Corporal Harvey Halpenny of the 3rd Canadian Division had endured in the trenches. It had been up and over, from one trench to another, month on end. Corporal Halpenny had the daunting task of timekeeper, it was his pocket watch they used, and he would stand on the left of the officer, and after the order to go over the top, would check the left side to see that every man had done so. The officer checked the right, and if any man was coward enough not to go over the top, on the order to do so, they were immediately shot, and it was Corporal Halpenny's task to carryout the order.

At half-past five on the morning of Easter Monday, 9 April 1917, the 983 guns and mortars supporting the Canadian attack, opened with a concerted and deafening roar. The assaulting troops, some lying in saps and shell holes close to the enemy line, others in the tunnels and trenches further back, moved forward in the cold north-west wind and chilling sleet, which swept the countryside on the momentous day.

Well ploughed by the bombardment, the loosened soil over all the western slopes of the Ridge soaked up the melting snow, which fell all through the afternoon and only ceased at midnight. The condition of the captured ground, which had assumed the consistency of thick porridge, mixed with strands of wire, stakes, trench-boards, sandbags and bodies, restricted the advance of the artillery to the Arras-Lens Road - now the only strip in the area where a horse could find a footing. These conditions would have prevented further exploitation, had such been intended, but the primary task of the Canadian Corps was accomplished. Vimy Ridge had been captured, now it must be put to a better state of defence, so that it could be securely held.

On 10 April consolidation proceeded, trenches were dug, machine gun emplacements constructed, and barbed wire entanglements erected. The Canadian casualties for the second week of April were 11,297, one of those casualties being Corporal Halpenny, who was wounded after he had reached the top of Vimy Ridge. A wounded German, who had pretended to be dead, shot him in the back. He did not have to pretend after he shot Corporal Halpenny, who turned and fired his .45's as he was hit, and both of his bullets found their mark. He wrote in his diary during his stay in the Field Hospital *"We formed into one line and walked slowly forward. After a few yards my friend was hit, then the man on my left fell, then another, then another. The German machine guns cut us down like ripe corn, and for the last hundred yards or so, my feet never touched the blood soaked earth, only the bodies of my fellow men. I just kept saying 'left foot, right foot, until I reached the top and went over firing."*

The hospitals were overflowing and Corporal Halpenny, who had never heard of Market Rasen, but was soon to do so, was packed on the beach with hundreds of other wounded and eventually sent to hospital in England where he met Eleanor May Hall. They fell in love at first sight, and after the war, he married the Market Rasen businessman's daughter, and joined the family greengrocery business.

With the ending of hostilities, the church bells rang out the good news that victory had been won and the war was over. Market Rasen celebrated, and Tommie Bonnett organised a great torchlight procession through Market Rasen, terminating with the burning of an effigy of Kaiser Bill on the De Aston Grammar School football field. Tommie Bonnett was a flamboyant character, and was well loved by the people of the town. He was a councillor for 20 years or more and he served the people well, but was often criticised by his fellow, jealous councillors.

Cross of Remembrance

Lincolnshire had a large part to play in the production of tanks in the First World War, with many models being made at Lincoln. Trench warfare brought forth new proposals for tracked armoured vehicles. Winston S. Churchill, First Lord of the Admiralty, backed the idea for tanks and this resulted in the formation of an Admiralty Landships Committee. This led in September 1915 to the construction of the first tank, called *Little Willie* - the tank had been born. At the end of the war in 1918, France had produced 3,810 tanks, and Britain 2,636. The French Army adopted the doctrine that tanks were a mere auxiliary to infantry. France's lead was followed in most other countries; the U.S. and Italy both assigned tanks to infantry support, and copied the Renault F.T. The U.S. copy was the Ml917 light tank, and the Italian Fiat 3000. The only other country to produce tanks by the end of the war was Germany, which built about 20. Time was to show that the Tiger was only sleeping.

The cost of the war was high. The Allies and Associated powers are calculated to have mobilized more than 42,000,000 men in World War One, and to have lost more than 5,000,000 lives, of which 3,000,000 were Russian and French. The huge war cemeteries in France and Belgium bear witness to this. At Market Rasen a memorial was erected in Chapel Street [see photo of the Cross of Remembrance] in memory of those who lost their lives in the Great War.

Life began to get back to normal, but it was never to be the same again for the little market town. The 1914-18 war was the turning point, for it was now only a matter of time before the harsh economic realities hit home.

There were soon signs that the town was getting back to normality, one being when the Post Office announced that it was to return to the same opening hours as those, which had been in force prior to 1914. On the leisure side, it was unanimously decided to go ahead with the plan for the re-starting of the golf club, after a meeting held in the White Hart Hotel in March 1919. Mr. Willey was ready to give permission for a golf course to be made on Linwood Warren. A committee was formed consisting of the Misses Barton; Miss Wilson; Doctor Torrens and Messrs T.H. Court; A. Drakes; B.A. Lowe; and P.J. Timms.

People again became interested in property, the time being right for any business minded person, to make use of the many building sites then available. There were many old buildings, that had stood derelict for many years, and nothing had been done with them with the war being up most in people's minds. James Nettleship, the auctioneer at Market Rasen, sold 'Braemar Cottage', a property at Middle Rasen, which consisted of a well built property, large outhouse, a boiling house with granary over, two pig sties, other buildings, an orchard and a garden, all for only £200.

CHAPTER 19

MARKET RASEN TRADERS IN 1926

Bridge into Caistor Road. Note the gaslight

After two decades of marking time, Market Rasen started on the downward path. In 1923 the Central Cycle Company announced that its turnover was insufficient for it to remain in business. The town badly needed investment to halt the downward slide, but it was not forth coming. The above picture shows the bridge into Caistor Road. The yard on the left is Burrell's the chemist yard.

Speaking at a tradesmen's dinner at the White Hart Hotel in 1923, Father Hengel, of the Roman Catholic Church, suggested that Rasen's gradual downward movement was not to be ascribed to any one cause. It was a setback, which was partly emotional and partly caused by a cycle of events over which a town like Rasen had very little control. However, nearer the truth was when he spoke about shortage of money, which was holding the town back.

Mr J.H.Nettleship, county councillor for Rasen, said that they shouldn't give way to pessimistic views when they had gone through the great testing time of the war. He went on to say that when the Conway Gordon estate was sold, the urban council should have boldly entered the market, borrowing money from London to purchase the town hall, the corn exchange, and the market place. He went on to say *"I believe that there is a living for everyone in a small market town like this if only we go the right way about it. So much depends upon your point of view when you are making a start. It's progress we want and if we go about it the right way we shall see Rasen going ahead more than we have ever thought to be possible."*

Mr. A.A. Padley, speaking on the same occasion, took up Nettleship's theme and said it could be that they had too many jeremiahs in Market Rasen. To the traders of the town he said, *"Cheer up. Be of a stout heart. Work hard. Keep steady. Results will then follow as surely as night follows day."*

However, at this stage inflation had not yet reared its ugly head, and turned everything topsy-turvy. In 1909 the price of wheat at Market Rasen market was on average, 36s 11d a quarter. In 1914 it was 34s 11d. In 1925 Mawer, Cooper and Burkitt, conducted a furniture sale for Mrs. A.E. Honneyman at the Elms, Market Rasen, and these were some of the prices: set of two arm and six small Hepplewhite mahogany dining chairs, £100; a serpentine front Sheraton mahogany dressing table, £55; Sheraton mahogany sideboard, £22; Sheffield plate candle-sticks £4 - 5s a pair. And so on. Prices of admission at the Market Rasen electric cinema in 1925 were ls - 6d and 5d. The pound sterling was then worth a pound. You looked upon it as representing a realizable and realistic standard of value.

In 1925 Messrs. Nettleship and Kelmnery, offered for sale by auction, 14 lots of freehold property situated in Market Rasen and Middle Rasen, for the trustee of the late Mr. Edwin Whelpton. Some prices were as follows:

Lot 1. - All that, well-built dwelling-house, buildings and grass land, numbered 192,193 and 194 on the Ordnance Survey map, containing 4.202 acres (more or less), situated on the Caistor Road, in the occupation of Mr J. Rankin.

Sold at £370 to Mr J. Rankin, tenant.

Lot 2. - All that Close of excellent GRASS LAND, known as Park Field.
Numbered 218 on the Ordnance Survey Map, containing 7. 246 acres (more or less), situated on the Caistor Road, in the occupation of Mr. J. Hankin.

Sold at £340 to Mr. A. Grebby, Market Rasen.

IN THE TOWN OF MARKET RASEN.

Lot 11. - All those 2 very desirable semi-detached VILLAS, situate in Chapel Street, in the occupation of Messers P.R. Copley and G.H. Timms.

Sold at £650 to Mr. Copley, tenant. Mr P.J. Timms subsequently purchased from Mr. Copley, the villa on the west side.

Lot 12 - All those 2 well-built Brick and Tiles COTTAGES with Gardens, situate on the Willingham Road, in the occupation of Messrs Chessman and Bartram.

Sold at £285 to Mr. P.J. Timms.

Lot 13 - All those 2 well-built Brick and Tiles COTTAGES with Gardens situated on the Willingham Road, in the occupation of Messrs Smith and Neal.

Sold at £205 to Mr. John Smith.

Lot 14 - All that excellent BUILDING PLOT (formerly a Grass Paddock). 1845 sq yards (more or less). situate in Chapman Street, in the occupation of Mr. R. Scupham.

Sold at £72 10s to Mrs. R. Scupham.

During the 1914-18 war, the value of the gold sovereign lost two-thirds of its value. Money values had always been maintained up to that point, and no one had given a thought to the fact that money would lose its value and come under fire.

Despite the gloom and doom, the little market town had all the qualities of a top market center. There were still many traders, offering just about all the goods and services that one is likely to ever need, all at top quality and right price. In just over 50 years, there had been many changes, and the commercial list from Kelly's Directory for 1926 shows the following Rasen businesses:

12 hotels, plus Nightscales lodging house at 10 Oxford Street; 3 chemists and druggists, Payne and Starbuck at 13 Queen Street, Walter Casterton at 4 Queen Street, and Charles Burrell in King Street; 3 doctors – Barton, Pank and Torrens; Dispensary & Cottage Hospital; Fire Brigade – James Sanderson Captain, Kilnwell Road; 3 banks – one being Midland Bank Ltd in the market place. Manager Bertram Lowe;

4 bakers - my relation George Footitt, being one at 56 Queen Street, and another being Burn Brothers at 25 Union Street; schools; blacksmith; the Market Rasen Brewery in Oxford Street; Maltsters – Gilstrap, Earp & Co; in Serpentine Street; wheelwrights; cattle dealers; marine store dealers; confectioners; basket dealer; iron mongers; painters; dairyman; gunsmith; even a horse breaker, John

Henry Spencer of 20 Prospect Place; auctioneers; tinsmith; veterinary surgeon; motor engineers; hair dressers – one being Leonard Hyde who was then at 5 Union Street; New Brick & Tile Co with works Willingham Road; dentists; cycle agents; plenty of boot and shoe makers and boot and shoe repairers; drapers; brewers, plumbers; butchers, there were 8 of them, three being, Mrs. Alice Mary Lancaster at 47 Queen Street, Arthur Cocking at 24 Queen Street, and Cottingham Brothers Pork Butchers at 18 Queen Street; coal and coke merchants;

Greengrocers, one being my mother and father – Mr & Mrs H.A.Halpennny of 54 Queen Street; tailors - one being my relation; milliners; timber merchants; house furnishers; watch makers; saddlers; cabinet makers; builders and stone masons; book sellers – Wyman & Son on the Railway Station, W.H.Smith & Son on Queen Street, and Samuel Fieldhouse at 37 & 39 Queen Street who was also fancy goods dealer; china dealers; insurance agents, refreshment rooms; fishmongers – one being Horation Mainprize & Son at 7 Oxford Street [who later turned one side of his shop into a Fish and Chip shop]; and, fried fish dealers – Walter Ward at 17 Chapel Street and Albert Kingsley at 7 Waterloo Street, who are the fore-runners of the English Fish & Chip Shop.

Not on the list was Mr. (Tin Hat) Hill, the racehorse trainer, whose racehorses were a familiar sight in the town.He broke in his horses in the paddock just past Fox's house on the right in Pasture Lane [known always to us as school lane. Dan Willey's (Joy, Freda and Ron) Farm [now (2003) the home of Tom Briggs and Family] at the end of school lane]. The big disappearances from the streets were the horses, which were gradually phased out, but for a long time continued in the villages.

In the 1930's C. Rowett had a Road Service Licence for stage and express carriages. From Oxford Street the Rowett Family started the first taxi service. Today [2004] Tony Blanchard of Blanchard's Taxis Ltd carries on the service his relations started

CHAPTER 20

RASEN IN THE DOLDRUMS

The above picture is of Queen Street. The cover has now gone from the railway bridge, and it does look much better without it. However, for many people, they felt that the sands of time were running out for the little market town, and in 1923, Dr. D.F. Torrens, the urban council medical officer issued a report, which showed what a threat might exist to the health of the people in the town if things continued to deteriorate. Dr. Torrens urged the town to mend its ways. The main points covered in the report were:

Water supply - good but low pressure at high points in the town.

Milk supply - most milk comes from the surrounding area and hygiene standards very low. [Milk churns were left for collection in our archway at 2 Willingham Road, and Mr Rhoades (Roady) paid me two shillings a week to skim the bits, chaff and other bits of dirt, from the top of the milk with the dirty ladle hung inside one of them.]

Bake houses - The five bake houses in the town are inspected quarterly and are fairly well kept.

Sewers - Foul air was being discharged from the manholes. The slop traps and house drains are mainly of bad design and badly laid. Closet accommodation is not improving. On the sewage farm the land is sick. The effluent bad.

Infectious Disease - The town had 5 cases of diphtheria in the past year, 9 cases of scarlet fever, one of enteric fever, 4 of tuberculosis.

Slaughter Houses - The three slaughterhouses in the town are inspected quarterly. They are fairly well kept but their situation and construction leave a lot to be desired. One public slaughterhouse would be much better.

Housing - No new houses have been built and no up-to-date record of the housing of the district is available. Many houses are of a very low standard, though none is being termed uninhabitable. Houses in Serpentine Terrace and Paradise Row are in need of extensive structural alterations. - There is a need for 12 or 18 houses at once to enable the worst of the existing houses to be dealt with.

The doctor's report was received at the monthly meeting of the urban council in stunned silence. The doctor was right and this clearly showed that Rasen's policy of keeping down the rates was getting it nowhere fast. The town was sinking in its own bog. The save-where-you can councillors now had the facts, which was clear proof that they had been too meek. The silence was obviously for a long time for very little was done about the report. Housing was the town's No.1 Priority in 1923, but nothing started to move until 1931, when it was decided that 24 new non-parlour type council houses should be built on a site on Caistor Road. But, there were second thoughts after it was decided that Market Rasen should be developed more on the lines of a community in a ring fence, and not just ribbon-like along the road.

Rasen obtained a provisional approval for the building of 24 houses, and the cost in 1931 was about £150 per house. It was thought at the time that this would meet the town's housing needs. But, after dragging on for over a year the Caistor Road building project was at length dropped.

By 1932 the Tradesmen's Association was calling for better and more car parking facilities. This had to be provided if Market Rasen was to expand and retain its market town function.

Meanwhile, Mr. Nettleship, who owned the manorial rights on the market place, wrote to the Market Rasen Mail saying that the public were taking it upon themselves to say this and that about the market place as if they owned it. He suggested they should mind their own business. Mr. Nettleship said that when pigs were sold in the market place, a councillor told him that it was a bit of a nuisance. Mr. Nettleship said that people who never came to him for business, used the market place as if they had a right to park there, and when asked for tolls they were terribly annoyed. Mr Nettleship drew attention to the fact that charabancs were stopping without leave in the market place, and children from them were scattering fish and chip papers all over the place. These were talking points of the time, and fifty years later this was again to be the issue, with the market place at the centre, quite literally.

And nothing changes, for in the 21st century, the market place is still an issue, for in July 2003, town councillor Alf Jones said that the market place wants looking at from top to bottom. He also said that he had not seen any accounts or figures about the market place, and that they should not be kept secret. The market place has been shady from Day One. Nettleship thought only for himself, not the town or its people.

Those who did most for the town and its people, were Mrs Caroline Fanny Smith, Mr John Nash, Mr Tommie Bonnett, Mrs Eleanor May Halpenny and Mr Arthur Cocking, the latter two as you will see in the following pages.

In the Thirties councillor Arthur Cocking was a great apostle of progress, and for Market Rasen it was often slow in coming. Up until the mid-1930's the town was lighted with gas from the Gas Works. It was Arthur Cocking, who by purchasing a Wold View site, and then passing it over to the Market Rasen council, at cost, got things underway. Years before, Dr. Torrens had suggested that Rasen should build at least six council houses and see how the town got on with them. To that councillor Cox said, *"We don't want to have houses on our hands."* Some, like Cox, could see no further than the end of their nose, and now with the chance to go forward, the town was still being held in check. Arthur Cocking told them to put their money in long-term interests, and what the town needed more than anything else, was more houses. Arthur used to say; *"You will never get anywhere while people keep on leaving the town- you don't judge a sausage by its skin."*

Years earlier Thomas Nettleship had spoken out in the 1870's about the need for larger type houses in the town. But he only spoke out because it would line his pockets. Little had been learned from Victorian Rasen. The town didn't want to continue any longer

with just little shopkeepers, but take part in the new technology. They decided they wanted to go in for industry and Mr. Trill gave the push when he started a manufacturing process. Meantime, money was still there to be made, for those who wanted to, and Mrs Eleanor May Halpenny did just that, even though had been hit by massive bad debts as people fled without paying her. Nevertheless, she found time [and money] to have a well earned day at the seaside resort of Cleethorpes, and let the train take the strain; and, [see photograph on left] we see her [on left] with her sister Sue relaxing on the beach, hence the footwear for the sand. Note the relaxed mode of dress and the hats of the period. What a pretty bow on Eleanor May's hat.

By 1931 the de-population of the villages around Market Rasen was in full flight. There was a drift away from the land just as Bishop Lee Hicks had forecast way back in 1913. At Market Rasen in 1913 the Bishop, who was a great friend of the farm workers and against the low wages, said: *"If you do nothing, these men will drift away."* It was now coming true.

The squires did not combine among themselves and they had no collective viewpoint. But, they did have thousands upon thousands of acres with little market towns like Market Rasen as centre points for the exercise of their power. However, the squires began to feel the wind of change blowing, with the coming of the motor-car and the new technology, and those who had hitherto ruled the people, were at last having to climb down. The big mansions such as Willingham Hall and Bayons Manor were too big and unwieldy, for the new conditions. The aristocracy was very much a waning force by this time, and their spell over the countryside was broken.

The biggest change was in farm ownership, which resulted in the transfer of agricultural land from the squires, to a new generation of farmers, who have become owner-occupiers. Two great agricultural depressions, the first and most serious one was in the 1880's and 1890's, the second in the middle term between the wars brought about the changes.

Men gave way to machines, and the new generation of farmers had to go in more for farm management, than what could be called traditional farm methods. This meant cutting the work force by some 50 per cent, and the overall effect was a reduction in confidence, which hit the market towns and Market Rasen was no exception. Things were so bad that Rasen people took the line they were bound to get better rather than worse. Hit by deflation, the cry was, *"where can we cut our costs?"* The horse was the first to go, and machines came in as farmers strived to cut costs.

Every type of farming seemed to be suffering at this period. In the period between the wars, wool went from 18 pence per pound in 1928, to 10 pence in 1930; and by 1933 was down to 6 pence per pound.

The great landowners gave no form of leadership, and socially the whole countryside changed within the space of a single generation. The big houses, like at Hainton, were much reduced in size, and many others closed down entirely. The Earl of Yarborough had earlier announced that he had to sell 8,600 acres at Cadney, Horkstow, Normandy- Le-Wold and Claxby, just north of Market Rasen. For the town, this meant the weakening of a long association with the Yarborough family.

Vin Bray being booked by Peter Manders

In Lincolnshire some 2,000 labourers were said to have left the land. The squires had put political and social interests first, and now they paid the price. Another who paid the price [see photo – taken bottom of Chapman Street] was Vin Bray, who you see being booked for careless driving, by 4 year-old Chief Inspector Peter Manders. By the way, Peter did go on to become Chief Inspector.

In 1927, prime minister Stanley Baldwin, conservative, was the guest of Lord Heneage at Hainton. In 1926 he headed the government during the General Strike of 1926. After a hard won peace it was again into battle, but this time it was on home ground between workers, their bosses, and the government. The strike ended after eight days, with the government promising another temporary subsidy, while a Royal Commission looked at the coal industry, which was in a nightmare situation. Baldwin spoke to farmers of Lincolnshire in Hainton Park in July, 1927, and he told them that no government could really save them, *"I don't know what the answer is and I know of no magic,"* he told his rain soaked audience, and the heavy downpour during his speech, caused Baldwin to say that the rain typified the whole farming outlook of depression and gloom. But, he was in safe Tory country, and even though the farmers didn't like what they heard, like idiots, they applauded the prime minister. Lincolnshire always did have a lot of sheep. However, for many, one of the great attractions of the day, was the appearance of Captain Malcolm Campbell with his famous racing car *Blue Bird.*

With Baldwin at Hainton was Neville Chamberlain, then the Minister of Health. He was later to become Prime Minister (May 1937 to May 1940) and famous for his little piece of paper, [that was only a shopping list] signed with fingers crossed by the Bavarian corporal *"peace with honour,"* (echoing an earlier Prime Minister Benjamin Disraeli) and. *"peace in our time."*

In the early 1930's nobody wanted the Wold land, and many leading farmers around Market Rasen faced bankruptcy. Land that was unable to be let was selling for £10 an acre or less. It was a far cry from the 1840's when Lincolnshire was regarded as one of the most highly farmed counties in England. At that time, Lincolnshire labourers were the best housed and best fed in the country.

Now all was changing, and as the Wold villages started to go into decline, an entirely new countryside was appearing. With the changes, farming for profit gradually came into the picture by the late thirties, and an agricultural officer became part of the Rasen scene.

The Wall Street slump hit other stock markets around the world. In Hollywood everyone was living off IOU's, and Clark Gable, [destined to visit Market Rasen] paid for his taxicabs with his signature on slips of paper. The giant collapse of money power, quickly spread across the Atlantic to a struggling Britain, where unemployment increased from 1 million to 2,500,000 between 1929 and 1931. People were on starvation level. In October 1930, wages in Lincolnshire were cut by 1s- 6d a week to 33s- 6d. The rot was eventually stopped with the start of massive government backing, to get Britain working again.

But despite all the gloom, money went further in the 1930's. A jar of strawberry jam cost 9d a jar, plums 6d a tin, coffee 2 shillings a pound, Swiss rolls 6d each, a bottle of White Horse whisky was 12s-6d, and a man's suit cost around £4. In 1932 prices at Market Rasen market were; eggs 1s-6d per dozen, butter 1s-1d a pound, tomatoes and grapes both 6d per pound, onions, blackberries and mushrooms all at 2d a pound. These were prices when the farming depression was still at its height, and had a marked effect on market towns such as Market Rasen.

It all depended on what you meant by prosperity, and with the depression hanging over like a black cloud, many Rasen trades'people were seriously wondering what was going to happen next.

During a formal visit to Market Rasen in 1932, Archdeacon Blackie, spoke of the difficulties of church administration, which were caused by the farming depression. He said that in 1930, as many as 49 parishes had failed to make any contribution at all to diocesan funds, and in 1931 this number had gone up to 54. *"I am deeply conscious of the worsening conditions which are resulting in so many farm sales and liquidations,"* said the Archdeacon.

Economically, of course, Market Rasen was in the doldrums, so much so, that in 1932, Lindsey County Council were persuaded to take a cursory look at the town's urban status, following a suggestion made by a committee, that certain small towns in the county should no longer retain their urban standing. But thankfully, Lindsey decided against putting Rasen in with Caistor, saying that the time for this had not arrived, and that for Rasen and other small towns, might pick up as trade improved.

CHAPTER 21

THE WAR YEARS

As the war clouds erupted over Europe, and the world was plunged into another world war, Rasen witnessed the birth of a new world, which almost overnight lifted it out of the past. The county prepared for war and above we see the Market Rasen Home Guard.

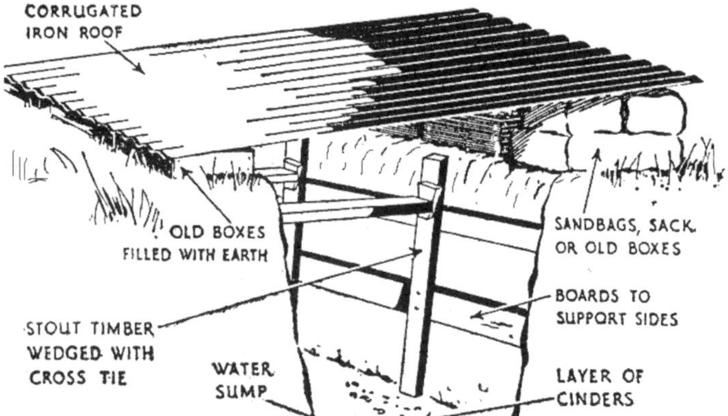

Anderson shelters were built in the back gardens up and down the country, but they never caught on in Market Rasen. Mrs. Nettleship had one built in the grounds of Manor House in Jameson Bridge Street, but it was only used on the odd occasion. Before the end of the war 2,250,000 Anderson shelters had been erected. That was for the upper class, for the middle and lower class, they had to make do with the 'Emergency Garden Shelter' [see picture on page 130] which was a 'do it yourself job'. The instructions advised 'that the floor of the shelter should be covered with a layer of cinders or old boards to keep dry. If possible, placed 20 feet from the building. A shelter made thus is, of course, not gas proof, but it provide excellent protection against blast and splinters from high-explosive bombs.' Yes, I think it would have done so, it was good; but for the Halpenny's it was under the stairs, for my father, it was outside watching, leaning on the archway doorframe, looking at the aircraft in the night sky.

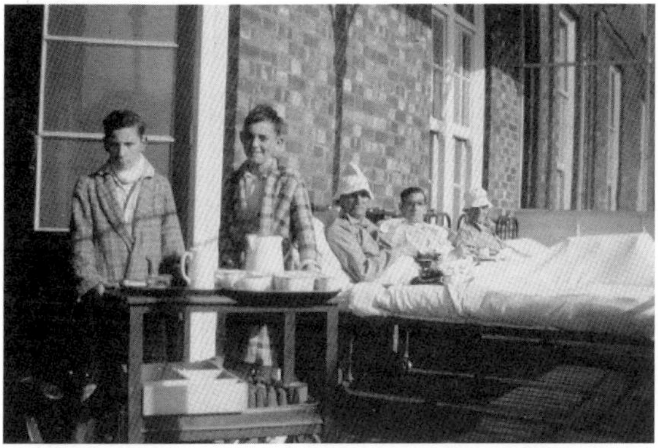

When war was declared in 1939, brother John – then ten years old, was in Shuttleworth Ward in Lincoln Hospital [see photo] under Sister Marshall who, lived in Market Rasen and kept an eye on him. Max Harrison the surgeon also lived in Market Rasen and worked at Lincoln Hospital.

Almost all the able young men of Market Rasen were called up for war service in the Army, Navy or the Royal Air Force. Many young men from Rasen joined the Lincolnshire Regiment, and reported to the barracks at Lincoln.

During the Second World War aerodromes surrounded the little market town of Market Rasen, and it seemed as if the whole of Lincolnshire had been turned over to 'Bomber' Harris. In 1941, the Tansley's farm – South Farm and Wood Hill [which are joined] – on the Linwood Road, was surveyed as a possible site for a bomber airfield. A surveyor [just one man] for the ministry spent a few days in the area, during which time he stayed with Mr and Mrs Ayre.

Despite being surrounded by bomber airfields, the town never received the might of Hitler's Luftwaffe. A few times the odd

bombs landed nearby, but that was as near as they got, and Rasen was fortunate not to suffer like nearby Grimsby. Gas masks [see photo for some of the types issued – the large one for baby] were issued to the town's people, Mickey Mouse ones for the children, but the town never had a gas alert. It was just as well, for the town was just too busy with bigger problems - like the Church of England. Market Rasen was one of the areas, which wasn't satisfied with the way things were going in the Church of England, and an area church meeting was held in the town in 1941, calling for what were called 'revolutionary' changes to be made in the new and challenging age.

The only real invasion Market Rasen received [most welcome I might add] was from those stationed at the nearby bomber airfields of RAF Hemswell, Faldingworth, which housed the Polish squadrons; Wickenby, Ludford Magna and Binbrook. The dashing aircrew were favourites with the local girls, and that included my sister Joan, who dated Wing Commander Guy Gibson of Dam Busters fame, a few times. All off-duty hours were spent in the town, which was in easy cycling distance from the camps. They were a mixed bunch of happy young men, Canadians, Australians, New Zealanders, Poles, and a few Americans, who were attached to Bomber Command or who dropped in from the nearby American base at Goxhill.

One famous person to pay Market Rasen a visit while at Goxhill was Clark Gable, the Hollywood Film Star. After Goxhill he went to an operational airfield in Norfolk and [see photo] Captain Clark Gable [on left] is seen sharing a joke after just alighted from the Flying Fortress following a recent attack [Yanks always in daylight] on the Nazi's great inland seaport at Nantes in occupied France in 1943. But while at Goxhill, he paid a few visits to Market Rasen. It was said at the time that he was dating Peggy Pank from the town. I saw him twice and each time he gave me chewing gum, a type that I had never seen before, but he was not chewing any himself [maybe not right with the ladies]. He could have had his eye on many of Rasen's young ladies, for there were many pretty young ladies at that period, who made the most of what they had.

Captain Clark Gable on the left

Facemasks were made out of table salt mixed with cold cream, and it was applied with a gentle circular movement over the whole face, removing the dead skin. Hair was usually washed in soft green soap, and as nobody had things like hair driers or heated rollers, it kept in pretty good condition. Blonde hair was rinsed in a solution of warm water and a tablespoon of lemon juice, dark hair in a vinegar mixture, and then sprayed with a little none-greasy brilliantine.

For many it was love at first sight and the town had many wartime weddings. One being as shown in the photograph on page 134. By chance, I said to my good friend Flight Lieutenant Tom Wardle, who had been bombing leader of 626 Squadron at RAF Wickenby during the war, that my Family came from Market Rasen, and quick as a flash, he replied: "I know it well. I was best man at a wedding there during the war." When he showed me the photographs [one as shown] it turned out it was my cousin, Marjory Egan, who had got married and Tom had been best man for.

A Wartime Wedding

Many Rasen families adopted the aircrew, who were obviously under a great deal of pressure. Mr. and Mrs Harvey Halpenny always had an open house for any of them. One of the many was an American called Johnnie in the American Air Force, but on special duties with RAF crew of No: 101 Squadron at RAF Ludford Magna [see photo bottom left of Johnnie in uniform, taken

in our back garden at Willingham Road.] Sadly he failed to return on 24 December 1944, his 73rd mission. The sad fact is he did not have to go, he offered to make up the crew for someone who was sick. Another being Sergeant Richard Whiting RAF of No:12 Squadron at RAF Binbrook. Richard always flew with his lucky mascot – a Teddy Bear, which he brought and gave to me after an incident, he would not talk about, and many years later when he loaned me his Flying Log book for research for my books, part was sealed and I gave my word not to open. His secret remained with him. You can read about Sergeant Richard Whiting's and Flight Lieutenant Tom Wardle's wartime escapades, along with many other true stories in my book *Bomber Aircrew in World War II* [ISBN 1-84415-066-6].

Some of the evacuees with members of the Halpenny Family

The Halpenny Family at No: 2 Willingham Road also took in evacuees that no one else in the town could handle. They were Joe the Spaniard, three Belgium lads, and Evene from Guernsey. Paul Fields from Linwood put forward Mrs. Halpenny's name, and they settled in well. Paul Fields sent many evacuees to 2 Willingham Road for the day, and Eleanor May fed all of them. Then, after tea, they would cycle back to Linwood to sleep. Mrs Halpenny never received any payment for having them. Not one-penny piece, and no thanks from anyone.

For many aircrews, Market Rasen was their last place on this earth that they saw. This was so for Pilot Officer Alfred J. Dickinson of the Royal Canadian Air Force [see photo on right], son of Alfred Ling Dickinson and Lela Dickinson, of Windsor, Ontario, Canada. On the night of 12-13 August 1944, 379 Lancasters and Halifaxes, struck at Brunswick, where important elements of the enemy's ordnance industry were located. Air-gunner in one of the Halifaxes was Pilot Officer Dickinson, who had visited Market Rasen and 2 Willingham Road only a few days earlier, and was now on route for Brunswick. Cloud was so heavy that no attempt was made to mark the target with flares. The raid was not a success, and sadly, Pilot Officer Alf Dickinson's bomber was shot down. He was buried in Kiel War Cemetery [see photo on left.]

The war seemed a long way from Market Rasen. But nearer home there were problems, and a major issue was for the people living on the Wold View housing estate, who had found flies in their water supply. They turned on the tap and got half a cup of water and half a cup of dead flies. This caused a real scare in the town. Doctor Torrens said that as a temporary measure, all tap water should be boiled before being used for domestic purposes.

With their husbands and loved ones away fighting the war, the people left behind suffered from the torrent of regulations and so-called advise churned out by bureaucrats in warm, plush offices, who had no shortage of paper for all their

Said one farmer, *"I expect just about every official return for farm stock would show pigs having poor litters, and lambs officially not born."*

As the war neared the end, Italian and German prisoners of war were housed in the town and at Willingham Hall. Some Italian PoW's were at Blakey's Mill in Jameson Bridge Street, and I spent many happy hours at the mill with the Italians, and got my first taste of real, homemade spaghetti. We went rabbiting and mushrooming on the racecourse with Sergente and a few other Italians The Italians, many of whom [such as Sergente – see photo on right] were in the care of Eleanor May at 2 Willingham Road, where the photo is taken in our back yard. After the war many settled in and around Market Rasen.

Prospect Place

Waterloo Street

Linwood Road

For years the sky over Market Rasen was full of the sound of heavily ladened bombers, as they struggled to gain height, circling, climbing, circling again. This would go on for about two hours and then came the silence, until the lucky ones, started returning home. With the war over, the skies were silent - it was a silence you could hear. On VE-Day, Market Rasen - like others up and down the country - held parties [see photos –Top: Prospect Place; Middle: Waterloo Street; Bottom: Linwood Road area – Brian Ayre second row, second from right] to celebrate the end of the war in Europe.

But there were still the Japanese, but not for long, for the dropping of the atomic bombs on Japan quickly made the Japanese surrender, and the end came with VJ-Day on 15 August 1945.

But as the victory bonfires faded away, it soon became clear to the war-ravaged Britons, that victory didn't mean the end of rationing. Millions were now returning home expecting to find a new world arising from the ashes, but for many it was not what they expected. The dreams of so many were shattered, when returning soldiers; sailors and airmen came home to Blighty. What they had been fighting for seemed worthless in the light of Britain's post war condition. Austerity was the name of the game, for homecoming heroes, and many told to 'Bugger off' when returned to their old jobs. Thankfully, this was not so much the case in Rasen.

Those from the war returned with their pinstripe demob suit, any colour as long as it was either brown or blue pinstripe or grey chalk stripe, a shirt and two loose collars, studs and a pair of cufflinks, two pairs of socks, a pair of shoes, a tie, a raincoat or Raglan overcoat, and a trilby hat. The whole lot was valued at around £21. They also had a gratuity and demob leave pay.

But some came out with more, and brought home with them their wartime brides. One to come to Rasen was a very beautiful German fraulein called Hannelore Chistel Dupont [see picture of Hannelore in Germany getting ready for the big day. She is also on the cover of the book with her puppy that replaced their Alsation that was killed by the Gestapo] who had married Sergeant Derek Halpenny in Germany, and was now Mrs. Halpenny. They settled in Rasen after the war. Sadly, Hannelore, who was liked by everyone in the town, passed away in November 1959.

Hannelore

In May 1945, the coal ration for the ensuing year was fixed at 50 hundredweight, and that had to last for a whole year. The sweet smell of victory in Europe quickly turned sour, when basic food rations in Britain were cut. The weekly bacon ration was reduced from four to three ounces, lard from two to one ounce, and twopennyworth of the week's meat ration, had to be taken in corned beef. A few people resorted to horsemeat.

During the war, rationing was accepted as a way to topple Hitler. But once the Germans were defeated, the people found it harder to swallow. The men home from the war now saw the appalling privations suffered on the home front during their absence. The women of Market Rasen - along with their counterparts elsewhere in Britain - had gone without, and struggled to keep the home together.

At 2 Willingham Road, Eleanor May organised it very well, for still had contacts from the greengrocery shop, we also had a large back garden and allotments that supplied more than our needs, even after feeding all the Servicemen and women and the Belgium lads; and brother John was now working at Burns Brothers bake house [see photo on left], for Windy burns a good friend of the Family; so never short for bread or cakes etc. The photograph taken just outside the bake house door, from left to right: Nick Hall [cousin] Eileen Hannath, Sylvia Slight [one of the 5 beautiful Slight girls, she married Les Douse], and brother John, fresh out of hospital. I will just mention that people who worked in bake houses had their hands inspected [at Burns by the Boss and by inspectors] for dirty fingernails. I speak only for Burns Brothers at all times for their hands and fingernails were clean at all times. We also got tea chests full of goodies from Canada. So, Eleanor May helped out all her Club customers during the war years, and none were ever short or went hungry, bread rationing was never a problem. Talking of her club customers, Frank and Tilly Burks, were good customers and good friends of the family. So that I could have 5 comics each week, the Beano, Dandy, Radio Fun, Knockout and Film Fun, Eleanor did a deal with Tilly, that being that they could have them on Saturday morning at half-price. Mike Burks or Pat his sister was always at our house early Saturday morning, and so I had to have read them by then. The comics I always had to keep clean and new.

It was good business for both Families. Mr Hancock, the headmaster, told my mother not to let me read comics (bad influence and all that), but I liked my comics and collect Film Fun annuals, and by very good fortune, later in life as a young man, I got to know Stan Laurel himself, who became a good friend and telephoned me weekly, but that is another story.

Post war prices were; 1 lb beef brisket, 7d; 1 lb tea, 26d; quarter of coffee, l0d; 1 lb bacon, 8 ½ d; 1 dozen eggs, l2 ½ d; l lb margarine, 3 ½ d; l lb butter, 62d; l lb cheese, 5d; 7 lb potatoes, 7d; and a pint of beer, 6 ½ d; and 20 cigarettes, 16d.

It now seemed one crisis after another, but the most severe blow, was the announcement, that from July 21 bread was to be rationed. Then, in November 1947 everyone was up in arms about potato rationing. They remained rationed until April 1948. The following March clothing no longer needed coupons. It had been a struggle to remain decent on the 48 coupons allowed. A woollen frock costing £3- l3s- 6d was 11 coupons; a woollen skirt was 16 shillings and four coupons. A pair of shoes at £1- 2s- 6d was nine coupons.

Bread rationing ended 29 July 1948, and sweets were de-rationed in May 1949, but rationing was reintroduced three months later, ending finally in February 1953. Tea rationing ended in October 1952. Butter, margarine and cooking fat came off ration in May 1954, and finally, meat and bacon rationing ended in July 1954 - over nine years after the war had ended.

As the dust settled it was a time to reflect on the terrible price paid over six long years of the bloodiest war in the history of man. By the time it ended, 54,800,000 men, women and children were dead. The total British casualties were: 357,116 killed including 264,243 in the armed services. In the United Kingdom 457,000 houses were destroyed and 4,073,000 damaged. 1,267 schools were badly damaged and 4,275 less seriously. Thankfully, Market Rasen town came out of the war unscathed, but many brave men failed to return and some returned with lasting wounds and terribly shocked, and received little or no help.

Germany suffered, and in Hamburg alone, 37,554 were killed, and the town almost obliterated. All major towns received the might of Bomber Command, and at the end of the war, were just heaps of rubble. In Germany, 2,700,000 houses were destroyed and 1,300,000 damaged beyond repair.

CHAPTER 22

POST WAR FARMING

Winston Churchill won the war, now the Attlee Labour government would try and win the peace; so, let us open the post war farming chapter with a 1950's view [see photo above] of the Market Rasen cattle market. George Brown, in his new post as Parliamentary Secretary to the Ministry of Agriculture, decided to make one of his opening speeches to farmers at Market Rasen. George pulled no punches and he made it clear that he had no time for those who regarded farming just as a way of life. He wanted results.

George Brown was in favour for higher productivity, and wanted to see efficiency on the farms, and efficiency, which was well rewarded. He said: *"Before we came into office, Lord Woolton and Mr. Hudson have been giving you post-dated cheques, promising that they would be cashed after the war. Such cheques were handed out in the first war, but they always came back again marked 'Refer to drawer.'"*

At this period the crops of Lincolnshire were: wheat being one of the most important crops grown. Barley, which had much shorter roots than wheat, can be grown on the thin soils of the Wolds. It could be sown in the spring, on turnip land, where sheep have been fed during the winter, and when harvested, easily transported to the great brewing centres such as Burton-on-Trent, Newark, Nottingham and, to the Malt Kilns at Market Rasen.

Although the oats crop was not as important as wheat or barley, a considerable amount was grown, taking its place in the rotation of crops. 'Rotation of Crops', was very important, for if the land was always planted with one kind of seeds, it gives worse and worse yields. This is partly because the same crop keeps taking out the same substances from the land, partly because it becomes subject to diseases and pests, and partly again, because it makes weed destruction more difficult. So farmers changed their crops from year to year. It is a very different story today.

Other crops grown in Lincolnshire being peas and beans, then mostly grown in the Fenlands. In winter, sheep are often fed on turnips, swedes and mangolds, so where sheep were most common on Wold farms, much land was given over to these crops.

SCHOOLBOY LABOUR ON THE LAND.

Ministry of National Service,
Westminster, S.W. 1.
20th May, 1918.

To the Editor.

Appeal to Parents, Head Masters, and Boys.

Dear Sir,

The military situation has necessitated calling up a large number of agricultural labourers, which will seriously deplete the available labour during the coming Hay, Corn, and Potato Harvests. It is of vital importance that the harvest of these crops should be successfully secured this year. This success will depend largely upon boys at public and secondary schools who have reached an age that will enable them to do useful work on the land.

The extent to which farmers are counting on their help is shown by the fact that demands for over 17,000 boys have already been received at this Ministry; and there is no doubt that these numbers will be largely increased when the full effect of the calling up for military service has been appreciated by the farmers. Of these numbers, not less than 3,000 will be required during June and July, and a further 3,500 are needed for October, for potato-lifting, if suitable accommodation can be arranged.

In view of the above facts, I am reluctantly compelled to appeal to schools to release during term time such groups of boys as may be necessary for getting in the harvest. This is a time of national crisis, and the ordinary considerations of education have not the same force as in normal times. As I have pointed out, it is necessary to provide men for the Army, and it is necessary to provide labour to take their places on the farms, and I must urgently appeal to parents, head masters, and boys to give all the help they can.

In view of my representations as to the urgency of the national need, the President of the Board of Education concurs in this appeal, and is issuing a circular on the subject to Secondary Schools in England and Wales.

All offers of service must be made through the Head Masters of the schools. Head Masters who have not already received the regulations, and who can offer boys of 16 and over, should communicate with this Ministry.

I am,
Yours faithfully,
A. C. GEDDES.

In the Fens and the Isle of Axholme, potatoes were the root crop usually grown instead of the turnip. Every year large numbers of women and children came from the towns into the country to gather in the potato harvest, for it was then not possible for it all to be done by machinery, and so required plenty of cheap labour.

The school attendance officer had come into being somewhere about 1875. But for non-attendance in the early days, it was easy to plead that the local farmer was short of labour, and the truant would only receive a warning. School children have always been a means of quick and cheap labour for farms, and even up to the 1950's and 1960's time off from school was permitted for potato picking. All schools - and that included the De Aston Grammar School, for many children were from farming families - in Market Rasen gave special holidays to children who wanted to help with the potato harvest, see photograph of potato pickers at work on farms near Market Rasen in the 1960's.

Rasen Potato Pickers

Sugar beet was another crop much grown in Lincolnshire, and is still very much so today [2003], but with only now the sugar-beet factory at Newark, the ones at Brigg and Bardney having closed, as the conglomerates genetically modified beet [not with my consent] takes its toll.

Other crops then grown were carrots, celery, mustard, flax, fruit - such as apples, plums and pears, flowers [notably near Spalding], and of course, the so-called seeds, which were used to provide food for cattle and horses.

The main animals on the farms were cattle, sheep, pigs and horses, the first three giving food, and the horses helping with work on the farm, but by then giving way to motors and tractors.

Once a familiar sight around Market Rasen, one of Marwood's steam engines

The sheep were originally of a type known as Lincolnshire Long Wools, and their wool was valued more than their flesh. In summer the sheep feed on the short grass on the hills, while in winter they are penned in turnip fields. While they are on the land, the sheep manure it with their droppings, and this, together with their constant treading, prepares the land for the next crop - which was usually barley.

The cattle reared on Wold farms were in winter kept in stockyards, where they were fed on straw, hay, clover, roots or beet pulp. The stockyards were then invaluable means of farmyard manure for the crops. Today in a changing world, of greed and profits, controlled by the big American conglomerates, it is all artificial fertiliser … killer chemicals.

Pigs were usually kept on most farms, and just about every farmer and farm labourer, kept just enough pigs to supply him with ham and bacon. The farm foreman also had a cow or two, and his cow had the best of everything available, so as to produce the maximum of milk and butter.

Many people in Market Rasen also kept pigs, and at the Rasen Pig Club dinner in 1950, it was reported that one person in every ten in the town still kept a pig. Mr. John Potts, sanitary inspector, remarked that this particular aspect of food production had always been well understood at Rasen, and that if there was one line, in which Rasen was thoroughly experienced, it might be thought to be this one of keeping pigs. It was very much so at the Halpenny home of 2 Willingham Road, for we kept 5 pigs, and I always had my one, which brought in my investment money. The ministry when ready collected the pigs, and you got your cheque through the post. It was simple. We had, up until the 1950's, always killed a pig for the Family needs. We did continue with the chickens, that gave a dozen or more fresh eggs daily, and these were increased during the war years, because of the vast number of people Eleanor May was feeding – Family, aircrew, evacuees etc.

An occupation, which spread very much between the wars, was poultry farming. Once the farmer would only keep enough poultry to fatten up for Christmas markets, and supply himself with eggs. Usually it was the farmer's wife who looked after the eggs and sells them on the weekly trips to market, and Market Rasen market used to have baskets and baskets of lovely brown eggs.

During the war, the value of food produced in this country rose from £285,000,000 in 1939 to £600,000,000 in 1944, when the farmers` supplied three-quarters of our needs. In the years between the wars, the farmer was neglected, for it was often cheaper to import food than to grow it in England. This is bad for the country and very much so for market towns like Market Rasen.

The evolution towards a new world proceeded very slowly, until the coming of the First World War. Market Rasen still had the carrier's carts, and the popular sick and dividing clubs. Many young lads had entered the postal service, while others went on the railway. Some emigrated, and in this sort of setting, there was bound to be a certain amount of experiment on the farms as well as a changing of method in production and marketing.

Since the early post-war period, there had been many more changes on the farms, with greater productivity and more agricultural machinery. The Wold farms have got bigger and bigger and bigger which resulted in cropping changes and livestock.

The period just after the war saw the downfall of the big houses, and during the summer of 1947, three Lincolnshire estates were sold within a short space of each other. Girsby Manor, so long the home of Sir John and Lady Fox was one, and the furniture sale at the manor was the family's last link with the area, between Louth and Market Rasen. Some time earlier than this, Sir John Fox had negotiated the sale of the estate privately to Magdalen College at Oxford. Included in the estate were the Girsby farms, together with the village of Burgh-on-Bain and outlying parts of Gayton-le-Wold and Ludford.

The prices make interesting reading: a Louis Philippe satinwood writing desk was sold for £21; an inlaid Empire display cabinet from the drawing room made £7-10s; a massive mahogany breakfront bookcase in the library, £135. Other bookcases sold in turn for £36 and £38. Vases of the Chinese middle period went for £6- 10s; and a pair of English china figures, 'The shy couple' fetched £7- 10s; a large dining table in mahogany on twin three-legged supports, £37; an oak refectory table £45; a set of eight oak dining chairs, £38.

Large items were almost impossible to sell. Nobody would bid for a big oil painting, 8ft by 6ft at the foot of the grand Girsby staircase *"Give me half-a-crown,"* said the auctioneer, but nobody wanted it at any price. The Girsby grand piano by Steinway was sold for £16 and two suits of armour went at £24 for the pair.

Another estate was at North Willingham and prices paid were very cheap, and it was very much a buyers market. For one grass field of two acres no bid was made at the sale, and nobody was negotiating for its sale. A grass field nobody wanted - such was the market. Willingham Corner Farm of 233 acres was purchased by Boston Deep Sea Fishing Co., for £4,500, doubtless as an investment, and at under £20 an acre. What an investment. Clump Farm of 128 acres attracted a bid of £1,400, but this was refused and the lot was withdrawn.

The big property and land sales taking place here, and elsewhere in Lincolnshire, meant big changes in landownership, and was an era of change. It was formerly the gentlemen of the district, who had the main say in the administration of public affairs. Now this primary position was changing, because so many squires were leaving, and waiting in the wings were the 'Big Brother' bureaucracy, to keep Mr and Mrs Joe Public in their place. Also starting to take a back seat were the parsons, who were at this period less important than they had been.

For many who returned from Military Service, the railway provided work, and we see in the photograph plate-layers [at work] on the railway, working up energy for the camera. They are, from left to right: Ted Crow [ex-army who sadly died due to Military Service]; Bob crow [Ted's dad, ex-army WWI –Mons]; brother John [ex-army]; Bill Goodyear, and Jack Deller [ex-army Italy]. The photograph was taken in 1950 just outside Market Rasen station.

In 1950 the weekly farm wage rate for the Market Rasen area was £5. There had been very little movement in the farm wage rate since the depression, and the low wages paid to the farm workers, I think, the main cause for the decline in the population of some out-of-the-way Lincolnshire villages. In 1936 the weekly farm wage rate was 32s-2d; in 1939, 34s-10d; in 1944, 65s-0d; and in 1947, 90s- 0d. From 1947 to 1950, the weekly farm wage rate had risen just ten shillings.

Speaking in Market Rasen Corn Exchange in 1957, Cyril Osbourne, MP, said that quiet little market towns, and the pleasing countryside lying around them, had at that time a much more assured future than some of the big towns and cities. *"I am not playing party politics,"* he said. *"I am looking at all this from a national point of view. The country faces the darkest winter since the days of Dunkirk. The trouble, I greatly fear, is that most of us are now concerned with consumption, not with production. We are too hell bent on pleasure."*

Of course Osbourne was playing party politics, and, it was a bit of a cheek for Osbourne to say hell bent on pleasure. That was not it at all; but, after 5 years of war and years of rationing, the people, rightly so, now wanted some pleasure and to look smart. Also, Osbourne seemed to suggest that inflation and unemployment, which was coming, wouldn't be a problem. He took farmland as a classic example of an asset, which would escape the paralysis of inflation and would indeed be sought after. *"There will be a rise in the price of farm land,"* he said. Farmland just had to rise for it had been very much on the low side. Mr. J.R. Burkitt, for instance, had had the Thornton Manor farm offered to him at £10 an acre and he had felt bound to say *'No.'*

Any fool could see that land and property prices would rise. In March 1965, for instance, Croft Farm at Middle Rasen of 45 acres, realised £11,900 when it was sold by auction at Market Rasen. Included in the sale were a farmhouse and buildings and a stockyard.

As land prices started to rise Mr. E.S. Carter, an officer of the agricultural advisory service, pointed out to farmers that if they were prepared to pay £200 an acre, as it now seemed there were people [these people being large Insurance Companies for investment] so ready to do so, part of the price in such an estimate of value, must be regarded as a write-off, because such prices were not justified by the returns which were being obtained.

But there was more to it than Mr. Osborne had earlier perceived. The discipline of profit and loss was one thing, but the waywardness of inflation, which was overlaid with scarcity values, was quite another.

Market Rasen, just like the farms surrounding it, had a gilt-edged underside, which those with foresight in the town might one day understand.

CHAPTER 23

THE RASEN MILLS

The Market Rasen mills, wind, water and steam, testified to the fact that in farming on clay and sand land in this area, there was a mixed farming economy running right through the structure.

During the 1880's flour started to be ground by steel rollers which were driven by steam engines and this was the beginning of the end for the mills which used stones as the means of their grinding operations. Brewing also started to use steam power and the technical advances seemed to leave little towns like Rasen far behind.

The four storey church mill at Market Rasen, designed as a warehouse, inevitably became a leading Rasen mill, which was worked originally by waterpower and later by a gas engine, which drove two pairs of grinding stones. For many years the Hill family were right in the centre of the milling scene at Rasen.

Just outside the town and believed to be the earliest post mill to be built at Rasen, a picturesque structure [see photo above] was erected about 1780 on the Willingham Road, just beyond Ketsby cottage. This mill occupied an elevated site to the south east of the brick pits, and in 1854 Thomas Hill, a miller from Ketsby, near Alford, purchased it. After about a century of continuous work, this mill was struck by lightning in 1895, and ceased producing any more flour. As the mills closed they were not replaced.

In Waterloo Street just beside the railway line was a 4-sailed tower mill, and there was another in Jameson Bridge Street, which was later passed to Mr. Blakey. During the Second World War, as you are now well aware, this building housed Italian prisoners of war.

The best Rasen mill was obviously the Tower Mill at the end of Lammas Leas Road. This mill had eight sails [see photo] and was therefore capable of making use of even the smallest breeze. Unfortunately this picturesque mill came to an untimely end, when it caught fire in April 1923. The mill had only recently been sold to Mr. Phillipson by Mr. T. Hill.

This was the second disaster for the mill, the first being in 1868 when the upper part of the mill, including the sails, had been blown off in a gale. During the reconstruction the mill was raised two stories higher, and two more sails were added to make it eight sails. It was then described as being *'the most beautiful of its kind in England.'* At the time when a six-sailed mill it was owned by James Bird Fowler, and was known as Fowler's Mill.

Fowler had been the last of the toll bar keepers at Middle Rasen. The mill was then sold to George Johnson of Linwood Road, who was a corn merchant and miller, and also, glass and china dealer. At that period, he had the corner premises in the market place as a selling point for his various business enterprises. After a quarrel with John Sanderson, a neighbouring tradesman who was a hairdresser, tobacconist and lamp dealer, in the market place, the Johnsons started up as hairdressers in competition to him. As a sideline [nearly everybody had some sort of side line], John Sanderson sold patent medicines in his shop, and the most popular was one called 'Composition', which he made up himself for the curing of colds. Fortunately, or unfortunately, as the case may be, Johnson didn't try to compete in this field.

The Rasen area had many mills, and late in the eighteenth century Tealby had two paper mills. The last remaining mill at Tealby is of course the Thorpe Mill, which seems to have been sold for £34 in 1722 - complete with kiln, equipment and utensils of the mill. In 1800 the mill was sold to Barnabus Walker for £320.

Along the banks of the Rase six mill sites have been noted, which can still be observed today. But according to records, there were as many as ten mills, including a leather mill.

As the wind of change gradually blew, the mill-sails ceased to turn and milling, which had stamped itself so fully upon the life of Market Rasen, was no more. The day of the country miller has now entirely gone.

Peck Mill was Rasen's first water mill, and it was approached by a little road, which was formerly called Foundry Lane, so named for the road to the foundry. The house facing you [once the home the Marshall Family] when you enter Foundry Lane was the western corner of the foundry site. The south side bordered the River Rase. The foundry has now long gone, and Peck Mill went out of production somewhere about the 1890's. For many years Mr and Mrs George Briggs and their Family – Henry [Tusky]; Ben [see photo]; Tom and George lived at Peck Mill.

Left: Ben Briggs seen here at Hamliton Hill. Ben was always at 2 Willingham Road.

CHAPTER 24

THE 1950's

WMC Outing

By the early 1950's, Rasen, and little towns like it, were still in a stop-go situation with the war still fresh in the minds of almost everyone. Nevertheless, the Working Men's Club – opened in 1925 in Serpentine Street – still had [rightly so] their outing [see photo above] and all looked forward to it. Harold Plumtree – 3rd from left, on the left, joined the WMC in 1928; Steve Godson is 2nd man from right, his wife Ivy next to him. Eddy Walker, at the back just behind Ivy, had the shop in Queen Street, and most Thursday and Saturday nights I went with him to the Dog Racing Track [night school maths] at Hull.

In 1950 Mr. R.L. Stirling, planning officer for the county, wrote to the Market Rasen Urban District Council, saying that Rasen, as well as certain other market towns, should aim at a gradual increase in facilities with the object of growing bigger. This was Rasen's big chance to put forward bold plans to increase to 5,000; but, the council let it slip away, and you will soon see why.

Mr. Stirling said that a population of 3,000 was needed if Rasen was to function satisfactorily in the future as a shopping and service centre. The county had held the view since the war that outward migration from the smaller towns of Lindsey should be checked, and that every effort should be made to assist a number of towns. Growth at Market Rasen was envisaged taking the population up from 2,218 to 3,000. It was also envisaged that Horncastle in 20 years should move up from 3,790 to 7,000. In 1983 the population was 2430 at Market Rasen and 4,102 at Horncastle.

But, with Rasen council dithering on the touchline, it was a case of 'would it go up or would it go down?' The answer for many was clear, and it came to a head, when on Saturday, 7 October1950, the Market Rasen Mail splashed across the front page, the crisis which could be no longer denied. Mr. R.V. Beckett was quoted as saying: *"Look at the roads! Look at the footpaths! Smell the sewers! We feel that at last the time has come for strong action."* The Chairman, Councillor W. (Jim). Walsham, J.P., summed up. *"To put it vulgarly,"* he said, *"we're broke."*

The town was broke because of bad management from the council. None of those on the council were broke; indeed, most were doing well, and Jim Walsham [credit due to him I might add] had plenty of 'lady friends' for each day of the week, for Jim it was not just ' Girl Friday' … and they are not cheap to run.

However, at that period, Market Rasen was not the only threadbare town; the nation had many Market Rasens, the only difference being, the course of action taken by the Market Rasen Urban District Council. Faced by the choice of starving or strangling, they voted, by eight votes to three, to put an end to it all, jumping at the painless method discovered by its clerk, and instructing him to apply for 'de-urbanization' and delivery to the custody of the neighbouring rural district of Caistor. A town cashing in its chips was unbelievable - urban districts often aspire to become boroughs, boroughs yearn to be county boroughs - but a town that wants to be a village! The town that Dickens pronounced *"the most sleepiest town in England,"* now acquired yet a further title to fame, by becoming the first town in recent British municipal history, to make official application to be reduced forthwith to the rank of a village.

Why? The schools were all first class and doing well. [See photos of De Aston Grammar School – 1948, young Halpenny sitting front row, 3rd left [as looking] of Mr Clews, the Headmaster – page 80; and Sheffield Manor School – 1949, Miss Gledhill 5th from right middle row – page 179].

In the autumn of 1950, time caught up with Market Rasen council. To the council, meeting as usual in a rented room, the town clerk voiced the brutal truth: *"What have you to lose? You own nothing. You have no offices. You certainly have a refuse-collecting vehicle - but there is a loan on that. Besides that you have a few wheelbarrows, a few spades, a little place at the corner of Mill Lane, and the mortuary. I do not know what else you have."* I will tell you what else the town had ... it had an ambulance, and the Rasen ambulance staff. I joined the St.John's and did racecourse duties – last jump on the wood turn – and ambulance duties with Freddie Harrison.

Rasen ambulance staff proudly pose in front of their ambulance. Mrs Robbins [wife of Vic] is centre front

Certainly the situation looked bleak for the town, the roads which had been un-repaired for years, continued to go un-repaired; the drinking water supply, although now almost fly-less, many times failed to muster enough pressure for the Wold View council houses, but that is the fault of the council, for it had incautiously placed upon a slight slope; the cracked old sewers, let in so much water, that the sewage works ran up an enormous electricity bill pumping it out, and they stank to high heaven.

By the turn of the century many houses had water closets, but many old outside privies continued in use right up until after the Second World War. The 'night-soil', as it was so-called, was collected at night by horse-and-cart, and two handlers, and it was applied to the fields. The 'night-soil' was thought to be very beneficial and put some colour in the carrots. One night during the summer of 1950, the night-soil horse and cart was outside Sandersons in Queen Street, near the railway bridge, when Dick White and Taffy James tipped up the 'dilly' cart, and its contents went all over the road. The people in the Queen Street, Willingham Road, Oxford Street area woke-up to a smell other than roses.

The town sewage system was by means of the Barrel Culvert, which starts in Linwood Road, passes under the railway towards Dear Street; with off-shoots along Oxford Street, Union Street, John Street, with two outfalls into the River Rase. The Barrel Culvert caused many difficulties where silting occurred.

Because of the endless drain on the town's finances, a proposal for putting up a public convenience was postponed after being accepted in principle. Councillor W.R. Walsham at the time said: *"A halfpenny plus a halfpenny equals a penny. But if you haven't got a halfpenny? People say we're lowing ourselves in Market Rasen. But we're sunk. What I'd like to know is how can you be lower than sunk."*

It all seemed very odd. To the passing eye, in fact, Market Rasen had everything a market town should have - except, perhaps, at that time a public convenience, and the right people in power. In 1950, no place ever seemed more permanent, than this compact little market town with its rows of shops along King Street and Queen Street, and its church and cobblestone square. The 1950's were the heyday of the Women's Institute, and the photograph shows the Market Rasen WI outing in 1957 to Wedgewood at Stoke-on-Trent. By the year 2000, well over 4,000 communities no longer have the WI.

How had it happened? The blame must lie at the door of the councils, coupled with Market Rasen's misfortune. As the town clerk had said: *"You own nothing."* When the Town Hall came on the scene, it was built - and owned, by private enterprise. When the moving pictures came, the Town Hall became the Town Hall Cinema. The market place? When the manorial rights came up for sale, the council didn't want to buy. [How do we know that? How do we know it was not a carve up?] Mr. Nettleship, a local estate agent, quickly snapped up the prime properties, and nobody said otherwise. Strange … unless?

Market Rasen WI outing in 1957

In the 1950's the market tolls and the parking fees, which might have enriched the town, went to the estate agent's widow - Mrs. Alda Nettleship, who also owned the cattle market. They are today owned by Mrs. Nettleship's son Nicholas - still in private hands.

The council was always quick to blame the boundary carve-up, but that was not a problem. Nevertheless, it gave them the opportunity to whine and whinge. *"We're like Berlin,"* said councillor Walsham, *"We're surrounded. Only I don't think we're so well off."* You can say that again, for Market Rasen's penny rate brought in the princely sum of £45.

Over England as a whole, the average rate in 1950 was 15s-8d. Market Rasen was an unprecedented rate of twenty-five shillings in the pound - which, a local wag suggested, fully justified the issue of black-edged demand notes. It was to aid such hard-pressed authorities, smoothing out the many inequalities of the rating system, that Whitehall elaborated the system of Exchequer Equalization Grants, made out of national taxation, and awarded according to need. Market Rasen at that period received the sum of £1,764; or a 3s- 6d rate, which just sufficed to keep the town tottering precariously along.

Market Rasen Fire Brigade

The situation was bleak for Market Rasen in 1950, the year of reckoning, and as the rates threatened to rise to thirty shillings in the £, they sacked two roadmen. That left three, and foreman Vic Robbins, who between supervising road mending, doubled as local fire chief, the fire-engine [see photo – Vic Robbins first on left] fortunately, being furnished by the county. Vic also helped out at the Market Rasen racecourse on race days. Also, to run Market Rasen, two scavengers [the good doctor got his way], one sewage farm attendant and Charlie Smith, the sexton.

Photographed on the Post Office steps are, left to right, standing: John Sutton, Myself, Pete Codd; squatting: Gordon Reiney, Mike Fletcher (?).

Further cuts seemed impossible. The clerk, H.V. Berkett, a solicitor in the town, was only part-time and he used his staff and offices. Fine you may say, but it meant he had all the data of everything, held in his office [and you all know that with solicitors it is the case of finding the one good apple in a barrel of bad ones]; medical officer, Dr. R.J.R. Macredy, watched over the town for £55 a year; and W.C. Boyall, collected the rates as well as being registrar of births, marriages and deaths, and fuel overseer. While the council fought this out, the people of Rasen went about their daily business; and the local lads theirs…watching all the girls go by.

myself and Hannalore

For me, it was the Fabulous Fifties – plenty of money for those with brains and who wanted to work. Always time and money for a run out to Cleethorpes [see photo of myself and Hannalore at Cleethorpes] for an icecream and walk on the front. The jacket I am wearing is bespoke and the first one made with material that had a metallic thread [like on the £50 bank notes].

Market Rasen believed that the government was an unnecessary evil, and the town's local government office was Mr. John Potts, and for his duties as engineer, surveyor and sanitary inspector, he received the yearly salary of £495. John Potts was the government of the town, and when he wasn't in one street condemning bad eggs in his role of sanitary inspector, he was in the next, re-angling the pavement in his capacity as surveyor, or investigating a case of flooding in his office of engineer. He also had many unexpected duties as the local government official. There was, for instance, the week when Princess Mary visited Market Rasen. The rates hardly ran to items like bunting, so John Potts borrowed some from Mrs Margaret Bayes of the Gordon Arms Hotel, and some from the next-door urban district council. Market Rasen supplied the ladders, and Vic Robbins.

In a town where two-thirds of the houses had no inside taps, and 'closet conversions' proceed at the comfortable rate of seven a year, John Potts role as public health officer was very demanding. As the 'government' of Market Rasen, John Potts was very much a solitary person, and very much in the firing line with the towns' people.

Because of the uncertainty and the wish for the town to become a village, Market Rasen was a topic of conversation. The B.B.C. broadcast that Market Rasen possessed only two wheelbarrows and four spades. The town was like a scene from a Mack Sennett comedy film and the council were the main players. The town was ripe for many comic stories.

People who did not know the truth were saying: *"The town was an eighteenth-century 'rotten borough' that had somehow survived, petrified into the twentieth century."* The people were not rotten only those from the County Council and some on the town council. Most people of Rasen were good-natured and hard working. The cinema now offered an enjoyable night at the pictures [see photo] and was well received.

But it had not always been like that, and it was Market Rasen's misfortune, rather than Market Rasen's fault. It had not received help or support from the landed gentry; and most of the council were there for their own ends, not the town. Only Mrs Margaret Bayes of the Gordon Arms voiced for the people.

As stated, in the autumn of 1950 it was decision time for Market Rasen, and the county council's inquiry had to admit, it was a huge problem. Alone, Market Rasen's penny rate brought in £45. But, throw in with the neighbouring Caistor rural district, and for the combined area, the same penny rate raised £224-15s- 9d, a sum that you could do things with. But could you? You still have the same dullards in power.

Confronted by such powerful arithmetic, the councillors rubbed their hands and hastily swallowed their pride - with one exception. The exception was [surprise, surprise] Mrs. Alda Nettleship, Market Rasen's only woman councillor, and by virtue of her late husbands' enterprise, the lady of the manor. Grey haired and energetic, it was made clear to her before the meeting, that Rasen must remain a town. She was told to *"Earn her votes or she is out, and all the world will know why. Rasen stays a town."* Mrs Nettleship made a lone last stand before the county council tribunal. During an interview [what a wonderful opening line] at the time she said: *"We councillors are elected to look after the town. It is our duty to pass on something better than we receive. Now, Market Rasen is the centre of this countryside. If you are the centre, things must be built up around you, isn't that so? There should have been a plebiscite. But I still hope the public will press for a town meeting*."

We had just won two world wars by standing and fighting, and Market Rasen that had turned out many fighting men over the years now offered up the white flag. But, Mrs. Nettleship was in a tight position, for behind the scenes, all was on the line for her; so, she gave them no chance to wave it. Harvey Halpenny, a Canadian Volunteer from the First World War, then married and living in Market Rasen, could not understand the idea to retreat, which in a way is what the town wanted to do. His duties had been to shoot anyone who did not get out of the trenches on the command to go over the top. The town was at war - with itself - and in a way it was a similar situation. The townsfolk did not want to be a village, and this was made very clear to Mrs Nettleship by Mrs Eleanor May Halpenny, who now had so very much in common with Mrs Smith.

Thankfully, the minister who returned a point blank 'No' to Rasen's request to join up with Caistor Rural District Council at this time suspended its death sentence that had first been confirmed by the county. Aneurin Bevan, the Minister of Health ordained that Rasen must continue to stand on its own two feet. Mrs Nettleship's neck and career had been saved. She could go on as lady of the manor and chain smoker, go on smoking her 400 'Passing Cloud' cigarettes a week, which as a young lad, I fetched in packs of 200 hundred, hundreds of times for Mrs Nettleship from Steve Godson.

The Remembrance Sunday Parade through the town in the Fifties was carried out with pride. Leading the parade, Mrs Thornton, Mrs Bacon and Grace Hubbert. Note all the inviting shops ...proper shops, like Len Hyde and the International Stores, full of all nice things, good food, service and civility.

Market Rasen was a very well placed Market town and after all, balance sheets could mean anything or nothing. It was not as the pessimists had calculated in 1952. Pessimists are never more than half-hearted. When Market Rasen had touched bottom there was only one way out if the town people got down to brass tacks. And that was upward. The real people of Market Rasen were friendly and helpful, and in those days, one could hear the cheerful sound of people going about their business, and the many shops were a hive of obliging activity. The Clubs of Mrs Eleanor May Halpenny were booming, as people worked hard, they spent their money on clothes and goods for the home, which they had been deprived of during the war years. People were happy … it was, as far as we were concerned and

Eleanor May's many Club customers … the Fabulous Fifties. Business was booming.

Business was also very good for the Sweet Shops, and with so many, you were only minutes away from one, which sold everything in the lines of sweets and ice-cream. The Sweet Shops at that period were: Garnett's Sweet Shop in Queen Street. Mr Garnet made the ice-cream himself and went round the villages in a small van; Ivy and Steve Godson at 5 Oxford Street; [Steve also ran the Bookies and Tobacconist]; Jack Toyne in Queen Street; Mr & Mrs Len Hyde the corner of John Street and the market place; Knobby Clark's Tuck Shop in King Street; Pommy Sands corner Willingham Road and Prospect Place; Mrs McNally on Willingham Road. [She had a parrot on a stand in the shop, and if you touched anything before Mrs McNally came in from the back room, it would hop about and screech out *'They're pinching your sweets missis'*]; Kemps in Jameson Bridge Street; Buck Harrison's Tuck Shop in the market place; Miss Page's, George Street; Bill and Hilda Sellers, Waterloo Street; Mr and Mrs Johnny Duke, John Street; Mr & Mrs King corner Union Street and Chapel Street; Mr and Mrs Wilkinson corner Oxford Street and Serpentine; Webbs on Serpentine, opposite the Working Men's Club; and Mason's Tuck Shop at Crane Bridge, Willingham Road, this mainly for the boys at De Aston.

A true Rasen character was Harold Plumtree [see photo on left] who was born in Market Rasen in 1911. The picture of him was taken in the 1950's and he was still going strong in 1986. Harold lived all his life in the town – except for the war years, September 1940 to 1946, when he was in the army. Since 1916 he has been cleaning windows. In the early days *" It was then one penny and two pence a window,"* he said. The town gave him a good living and a good, happy, contented life.

As Market Rasen began to edge forward it was revealed that the town's waiting list for council houses had doubled and there was now a shortage. In its infinite wisdom the urban council had reviewed the housing position in 1952, and having decided that things were going too well, applied the brakes to the building programme. Now you see why the town shuddered to a halt, with such idiots in power who thought only for themselves. They strangled the town and brought it to its knees. They should have been on Gibbet's Lane.

Mrs Eleanor May Halpenny– photographed in the Halpenny Family home of 2 Willingham Road in 1951, the archway at the back leading to Willingham Road, with Bruce our Boxer dog and SS Jaguar car

Rasen councillors were still thinking in terms of a small town, and gave very little thought for the future of the town. Mr. Gordon Trill was distrusted at first by some of the town's people and the councillors, when he started making plastic boxes in the backroom of his hairdressing shop in King Street; but not by Mrs Eleanor May Halpenny who gave him support to go ahead, and I remember seeing dozens of his little trinket boxes at 2 Willingham Road, in the early days; when, peach and white were the only colours.

Gordon, having won a national contract in the plastics field, pointed the way to overcoming the town's post-war troubles. Mr. Trill's growing industry, Progressive Inventions Ltd., was looking out for houses for its growing staff. Mr. Trill thought that Market Rasen ought to be flying just a little bit higher than it had been doing. And, to back up his company's growth, Mr. Trill started to advertise for more staff.

The following advert was placed in the Market Rasen Mail in June 1952.

GIRLS WANTED
FOR WELL PAID AND
INTERESTING WORK AT
MARKET RASEN PLASTICS

Age	***15 - 40/-***	***weekly***
	16 - 45/-	***All***
	17 - 50/-	***Plus***
	18 - 55/-	***Contract***
	19 - 60/-	***Bonus***
	20 - 65/-	

Local residents preferred
Apply in person to
Mr. Gordon Trill, Progressive
Inventions Ltd., 16 King Street,
Market Rasen.

The advertisement shows the wages at that time, the average wage being £5 a week. Private houses cost in the region of £500 and a Morris Minor car £125.

The people of Rasen were beginning to feel that at long last the worst might be behind them. Advertisements appeared to persuade women to make more use of their good looks. Hairdressers were recognising that they belonged to a profession - the profession of beauty. In Market Rasen, A. Horsfield and Son, radio engineers, Queen Street, told their local audience:

"We now have a resident fully qualified service engineer for radio and television and we also have a demonstration room which we are sure you will find interesting."

The tide might be turning for Market Rasen.

The Fifties street scene of the town shows a hive of activity, the photograph taken from George Street looking east down Queen Street. All nice, clean and inviting shops. The people clean and smart – I wonder who the young Signorina is with such a nice smile? It is a scene of prosperity; and knowing from Mrs Halpenny's Clubs, it certainly was, despite what the councillors said, the town was good, very good, and all Eleanor May's Club customers were happy ... very happy.

Left: Mister Jim Batchelor who took over from Harold Plumtree. One of the most agreeable men you'll meet.

CHAPTER 25

RASEN RACING

Croix de Guerre winning at Market Rasen Racecourse

At any race meeting, you need to start with a winner, so let us open the Rasen Racing Chapter by leading in a winner … Croix de Guerre [see photo above], trained by Jenny Pitman [right of horse] in January 1986.

Two of my horses

For centuries the horse has had a place in the sports and pastimes as well as in the work of the British people. Very much so in my case, I have always loved horses, and had the right contacts for winners. As a professional punter [I explain the gambles in my racing book due out in September 2004]. I put on the 'hot money' for the Big Boys. I had 7 horses in training [see photo of two of them on left] at one time. The other photo is I with Bas Hales [see photo below] with one of Frank Wright's horses. Since the time of the Romans, Market Rasen has maintained its link with the horse, and therefore, only fitting that it has an excellent racecourse, which is the only one in Lincolnshire. Under the guiding hand of Victor [Luke, as I always called him] Lucas, who had been appointed Clerk of the Course and Managing Director after the war, the little National Hunt course went from strength to strength, but more about that in a moment.

The early racecourse was on Low Grange Farm, Middle Rasen, with entrance off the Caistor Road. The racing was like point-to-point racing, and there were no facilities for the spectators. Wagons were pulled into the winning post area and people stood on these, for there was no such thing as stands in those days … they came with Victor Lucas. The first recorded race meeting at Market Rasen was on Thursday 17 March 1859.

Horse racing started on its present site, situated on the A631 road just east of the town, in 1924. Four people were involved in the move, from Caistor Road to the east of the town for the racecourse, the chief instigator being Jimmy Nettleship, who, give him his due, was farsighted enough to see the potential in having a racecourse. With his silver starting pistol [today the proud possession of his son Nicholas] he was starter at the races up until his death on 11 July 1940. Up until the war there were only a few wooden buildings augmented by marquees; nevertheless, the racing was good, as Singlecote shows [see photo] when he clears the water jump with ease, in September 1926, and then goes on to win.

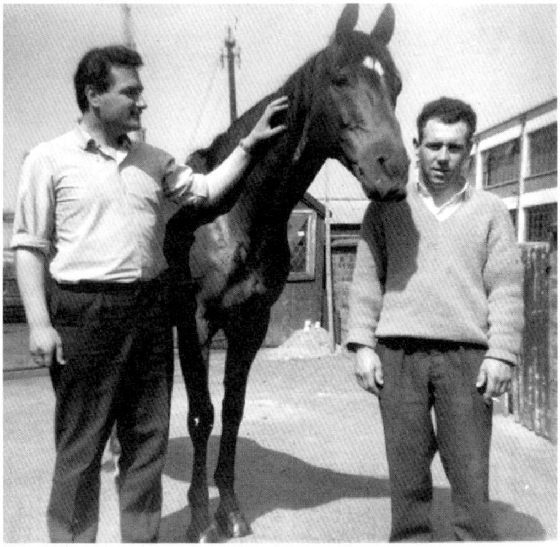
Myself with Bas Hales

During the Second World War the racecourse was requisitioned and used as an anti-aircraft headquarters. When the tide turned in favour of the Allies, its role became less important and towards the end of the war, many Italian prisoners-of-war were housed on the racecourse. A main form of pastime was rabbit catching and basket making with reeds from the nearby woods.

Singlecote at the water jump

After the war the mammoth task of clearing up began, and concrete foundations were drilled-up and miles of barbed wire removed. More than a hundred army buildings had to be pulled down, while others were purchased by the racecourse and converted for their own use.

The new-look Market Rasen racecourse, reopened on Easter Monday 1946, before a record crowd of 22,000 pleasure-starved racegoers. The record crowd due solely to the ingenuity of Victor Lucas. For that first race meeting after the war, petrol was on strict ration. However, farmers could get petrol and use in the motorcar if for business. This gave Luke an idea of how to get the punters to the races. He organised a farm sale near the racecourse on the day of the races. As he well knew, farmers flocked to the sale, which took about an hour. After the sale … the petrol used for business, they walked from the sale to the races. But if they drove the short distance, the police booked them for illegal use of petrol. That explains the record crowd of 22,000 racegoers. The starter was William Percival (Percy) Pepper, and [told here for the first time] the starting gate was a rope and elastic band.

Victor Lucas set to work to develop Market Rasen's racing potential. In a beautiful woodland setting, the racecourse had much to offer and Victor Lucas soon showed what could be done. Each year improvements were made and the course's reputation steadily grew.

The town became a hive of activity during race days, and all accommodation was fully booked, with jockeys and stable lads and all those connected with horses. Mrs. Halpenny at No.2 Willingham Road many times had to find room for three or more jockeys who were unable to find a place to stay. Many horses came in by rail the day before racing, and there was a special siding for the rail horseboxes. The town became a little boomtown on race days, as money poured in, and it gave employment to many people. Race days were always something to look forward to.

Once again, horses were owned and trained by Rasen people. The success of a locally owned racehorse, *Accurate*, belonging to Mr. Leonard Hyde, a Queen street tradesman, was a feature of the 1952 Easter Monday race meeting at Market Rasen. In a field of ten, *Accurate* won the hurdle race at 10-1. The attendance of 15,000 was a record for the meeting. The traffic hold-up was worse than ever known, a four-mile queue of cars extending from Rasen to Faldingworth.

Nice views of the racecourse

The course is an oval-shaped circuit of approximately 1¼ mile, and the horses are never out of sight during the running, whether one is in the Paddock or Silver Ring stands. Nice views of the racecourse [see photo] showing bend into the home turn, which in the early days 'unseated' [said with tongue in cheek] many a good jockey. The new £50,000 stand opened in the course enclosure in 1967 and was followed by new buildings for Tattershalls and members. In October 1967 Luke's wish came true, when the shareholders of the Market Rasen Racecourse Company, accepted an offer from Racecourse Holdings Trust Ltd; the non-profit making subsidiary of the Jockey Club, and by so doing, Luke had ensured the survival of the racecourse. Luke had told me of his plans, and when he told me it was done, I was so pleased for him. For Victor Lucas, each year had to be better than the last in order to attract more people, and better class horses. He was rewarded for the latter in 1968 when Market Rasen was upgraded from a category 4 to a category 3 racecourse, permitting higher prize money to be paid. Now the course can boast a stable lads canteen, landing strip for aircraft, children's playground, picnic area, free car parking and free race cards. From just two race meetings a year in 1924, there are now 18 race days a year … thanks to Luke.

Victor Lucas

Victor Lucas [see photo] attracted sponsorship and television became interested in this little Lincolnshire course, snuggled beneath the Wolds. Sadly, in 1971 Victor Lucas died. He had achieved his ambition to put Market Rasen on the map for racing, and offer the complete family a good day's racing.

But, with the mainspring gone, things did not have the same drive, and the television company pulled out [for reasons I will not say] from televising Rasen races. This was a blow, for it also meant the loss of some of the sponsors who came because of the television coverage.

Market Rasen racecourse owes everything to just one man … Victor (Luke) Lucas, whose foresight, drive, initiative, determination and enterprise, brought the little known racecourse onto the world stage of racing. He, and he alone, did that. Luke had to have the right yellow gorse for the hurdles, and the water jump was the main feature in front of the stands for all to see. Luke got more race-days, better racing, and televised races. He got the best grounds man – Pete Bontoft, who lived and worked for the racecourse, under Luke's guidance. A good team that worked. I kept Luke in fish [he loved finny haddock] boxes of it fresh from Grimsby, and he saw I always had Daily Club Complimentary badges. Luke was a very old Family friend, and in 1971, did the foreword for the book *British Racing and Racecourses* by Mrs M. R. Halpenny.

FOREWORD

It is indeed a privilege to have been asked to write this foreword and a pleasure to do so. I feel that in spite of the very varied and extensive literature on racing, much of which has been published in recent years, the general public on which we Executives so depend have little knowledge of the Turf.

I feel that one of the great attractions of our racecourses is that each course has some feature entirely its own, and that there is such variety from course to course.

In this book I feel that the many differing aspects are shown which will be of the greatest interest and value to our Owners, Trainers and racing Public. I consider this publication will be a "must" for all who are interested in the many situations which arise in Racing and will also be an inducement to those who have not hitherto gone racing to take an interest in that great Sport.

Chairman and Managing Director,
Market Rasen Racecourse Ltd.

Over the water jump at Rasen

Now in the 21st century, there is a woman Clerk of the Course, and sadly, she removes the water jump … that meant so much to Luke. The water jump is part of steeple chasing history … but not at Market Rasen racecourse.

CHAPTER 26

SCHOOLS FROM THE 1950's

1953-1954 Modern School

With such a happy scene, let us start the 1950's school chapter, with a school photograph for 1953-1954 Modern School. All the pupils looking happy and smart, so top of the class for the school photograph. The 1959-1960 school photograph is on page 177.

Changes were also in the wind for the schools, and sadly, many with new ideas were replacing many of the old well-respected Rasen schoolteachers. The Sheffield Manor School, run by Miss Gledhill [see 1949 photo with Miss Gledhill 5th from right, middle row, at end of chapter] was destined to close. In June 1952 presentations were made to Mr. A. Hancock, retiring headmaster of Market Rasen Church of England School. Replying to praise of him at a farewell gathering at the school, Mr. Hancock said of Market Rasen children: *"They are a grand lot."* Mr. Hancock was said to have been a firm disciplinarian, that I can vouch for, having had the cane many times, but it was just, and he remarked: *"Sloppy school discipline is the cause of much of the trouble among the teenagers today."*

At an inaugural meeting held in 1966 for the launching of the new comprehensive education project, Mr. G.V. Cooke, the then Director of Education for Lindsey, politely rejected the idea that a De

Aston School of 900 pupils was going to be too large for a small town like Market Rasen.

The stage was therefore being set for the opening up of a bold new chapter in Rasen's educational history. In the past, the schools fitted happily and successfully into the social environment of Rasen.

The idea that 'small is beautiful' as seen in the old De Aston Grammar School context, had its supporters, and rightly so for the De Aston was a great credit to the town. Mr. Cooke did not say at the inaugural meeting that Rasen schools had been getting bigger and bigger ever since the turn of the century.

1959-1960 Modern School

When Mr. Bruce McGowan, the headmaster of De Aston Grammar School left in 1964, he spoke of the importance of the growth factor, which had been seen at the school in his time. Numbers had increased from 255 in 1957 to 315 in 1964 almost entirely as the result of the increase in sixth form numbers from 22 to 70.

Growth had also been made at the Modern School. This school, then called the Market Rasen Senior School, started up with eight schoolteachers just before the Second World War. There was also a caretaker and three cleaners.

At the time of the name change to the Modern School, school dinners for out-of-town children started. In charge of the new school kitchen was Mrs. Marsh, who was paid £1 a week at the start for feeding 180 children.

But Mrs. Marsh found it impossible to cope on her own, so the Education Authority, appointed an assistant at ten-shillings a week. School meals were then 2½d per head. But if there were three children from one family the charge was brought down to 2d a head. Thus, three children from one family got their dinners for an all-in figure of sixpence. The children not only got a good hot meal of meat and vegetables, but were also taught to eat and sit properly at the dinner table.

In its early days the school catchment area had to be extended, because numbers didn't come up to expectations. But even when children from Hainton, Kirmond, Ludford and Normanby were brought in, the numbers at this school were no more than 192.

After the war two important changes were made at the Modern School. One, the school leaving age was increased to 15; and two, as a consequence of this, the school was organised on a basis of a 4-year, rather than a 3-year course.

This brought numbers up by about 100 to the 300 mark. New buildings were erected, new playing fields acquired, and the school truly began to take on a more modern look.

By 1948 the numbers at the Modern School had risen to 385 and this growth continued in the next decade, bringing this school over the 500 mark, and was an all-time high for a rural area school. With this expansion came a further building programme, rounding off a building scheme which could be regarded as taking perhaps 20 years or so for its full accomplishment.

Layout schemes are sometimes themselves full of limitations and anomalies. This became apparent when the Modern Schools became the new comprehensives. The De Aston also became a comprehensive school for both boys and girls, sweeping away the old grammar school traditions and old educational principles. Gone was the cap and gown master, and with it the respect. Gone also, after a time, the compulsory school uniform and cap. Out of the window went the old grammar school system, and the De Aston numbers shot up to about 1,250 with a permanent teaching staff of up to 55, and with part-timers, the number goes up to about 70.

Building work continued in 1972, to transform De Aston School, as part of the local move towards comprehensive education. The once proud De Aston Grammar School was gone. By the 1980's violence and drugs were commonplace in many schools, and in June 1985, University of London dons, Jean Lawrence and David Steed, accused schools - mainly comprehensives - of ignoring loutish behaviour. The dons said in The Times Educational Supplement:

"Not enough weight is attached to the seriousness of disruption in our schools. There are many schools where the price of peace is the acceptance by teachers of the simple refusal of many pupils to conform and learn."

The people of Market Rasen had unprintable remarks for the teachers, whose dress leaves much to be desired. I was informed that one teacher, with not a very stable mind [remember they are in charge of children] was found one day, trying to set light to a fire-proof carpet in the school library. The teacher was not removed, but stayed on; thus a clear case that the teachers banded together to save one of their ilk. The old adage 'Birds of a feather flock together.' Many times a teacher would enter class with a mug of tea or coffee in their hand to start the lesson. In the words of Bugs Bunny [who I am told refused the headmaster's job] *"What a maroon."*

Entering the 21st century, the market town of Market Rasen, has just two schools; the Church of England Primary School in Mill Road – the old Modern School – which takes children aged 4 to 11, and the other school is the De Aston, that takes pupils from aged 11 to 18. De Aston has some 1,300 pupils, including 260 in the sixth form. It is mainly a day school but still takes around 70 borders.

1949 class at Miss Gledhill's School

CHAPTER 27

THE TENNYSONS

Bayons Manor had long been a feature of the Lincolnshire countryside, but in such changing times the last squire of Tealby, Captain Alfred Tennyson d'Eyncourt, decided towards the end of the Second World War, that Bayons Manor could no longer be maintained, and in sheer desperation an offer reputed to be less than £50,000 was accepted from a London estate broker for the estate.

It had become more and more of a problem to keep up such a huge mansion. In the old days, with Tealby a poor village, there were plenty of young girls and men to enter service. In Charles Tennyson's time several boys were kept to run messages, stoke up the stoves, and see to the fires. One man was kept busy sawing and chopping wood all the time. As there were no bathrooms it was one person's job to do nothing more than to carry hot water to the rooms. Water was supplied to Bayons Manor from five springs. All the drains flowed into the moat, then into the lakes in the park. In 1900 there were 100 oil lamps regularly to use for lighting purposes. The sale of Bayons Manor brought to an end the Tennyson era, which had long been associated with Market Rasen.

During the later half of the 18th century Michael Tennyson moved from Holderness to Market Rasen, to practice as a surgeon. He pulled off the marriage of the century when he married the wealthy heiress of Claytons of Grimsby, and overnight he had all the money and power that he desired. The Claytons lived at Clayton Hall, where today in Grimsby, the General Post Office stands. What was their home close for their horses, extended southwards, and is now a supermarket and railway station. They also had many properties and land at Cleethorpes and Scartho. Let us remember, at this period; Grimsby was mostly open fields with a population of only around a thousand.

George Tennyson, born 1750, son of Doctor Michael Tennyson, married Mary Turner and they had four children, Elizebeth, Mary, George-Clayton and Charles. George Tennyson lived near the Caistor Road entrance to Market Rasen.

The wealth of the Tennysons' came from the success of the Claytons and was transferred via George, the son of old Doctor Michael of Market Rasen. With his wealth George Tennyson bought and sold property, one being the Elizabethan Manor House at Tealby, which had belonged to Lord Lovell and d'Eyncourt from whom the Claytons claimed to be descendents. George Tennyson was hell bent on building up an impressive fortune, and to do so was a man without very fine scruples [he was a businessman and out to win, credit do to him]. George, owning nearly half of Grimsby, and more besides, brushed Rasen aside. That did leave it to others, but no one took it.

George Tennyson was one of those who presided over North Lincolnshire's great age of improvement, but never for Market Rasen. Having his eye perhaps on personal and family advancement, the town of Market Rasen, had little to offer.

George was continually pressed by his son Charles to take the name d'Eyncourt, but he did not want to do so, saying he was proud of the name Tennyson. George, having moved from Market Rasen to the Manor House at Tealby, was worth £14,000 a year at this period He started to make his mark, and built a road bridge at the foot of Bully Hill, constructed Paper Mill Lane, made a minor road to Walesby by levelling the land at three points on this road; made Castle Farm look as much like a castle as he could, and he added the castellated top to the building. The wood near Castle Farm, called Bedlam, was where the hospice of Bethlehem had once stood.

George would not give way with the name. However, after he died in 1835 his son Charles got his wish, and changed his name to Charles Tennyson-d'Eyncourt.

The Tennysons of Bayons Manor, let us remember, were of Market Rasen, and when one speaks of the two branches of the family, one refers to the two sons of old George of Market Rasen. These were the Rev. Doctor George-Clayton Tennyson, the Somersby branch which produced Alfred, the great Poet Laureate, and Charles, the parliamentarian of the House of Commons, when it passed the great Reform Bill, and who, of course, built Bayons Manor.

Up to the time of George's death, the Tennyson family pew was always kept up in style in the church at Market Rasen. George had owned property in the centre of Rasen and also just outside the town. In the eighteenth century the Astons had been the main landowners both at Market Rasen and Linwood, and when the Aston property was disposed of round about the time of the Battle of

Waterloo, it would doubtless have been easy for George Tennyson to buy up this estate and add it to his Tealby holdings.

But George was a seller rather than a buyer at Market Rasen, for it made more sense to have in the district a family of the standing of the Conway Gordons, linked as they were with the higher aristocracy.

George Tennyson was a man for power, and one can still read George's letters about his purchase of Grimsby properties, and about the thinly disguised bribery, to which his agent resorted at election times, nothing has changed. Many of these letters were written from Market Rasen, which would of course know nothing about them.

For nearly forty years Charles was in Parliament, first in what could be regarded as the family seat of Grimsby, then as the representative of one of the new London boroughs. Charles, in due time received the major part of old George's fortune, and was also the inheritor of much of the family's Lincolnshire influence. Charles was proud of his own lineage.

The building of Bayons Manor was the symbol of the new Tealby. At that period, the village of Tealby was largely the abode of labourers, who worked for about a shilling a day. Tealby was a village, which was brought up in poverty, and was kept at the bottom of the social ladder. This could have been one of the main reasons why George Tennyson bought the Tealby property. Bayons Manor was a mansion fit for a nobleman. However, neither Charles himself, nor the picture book Bayons Manor, quite attained the role portended for them.

The Somersby branch of the Tennysons started with George-Clayton Tennyson, born 1778, married Elizebeth Fytche, and they had 12 children. Their fourth child was Alfred who was born on 6 August 1809 at Somersby rectory in Lincolnshire. Alfred, with his two brothers, Frederick and Charles, was sent to Louth grammar school, but he was unhappy and he left in 1820. He spent much time at his grandfather's house in Market Rasen. Sadly, in 1824 the health of Tennyson's father began to break down, and he took refuge in drink. He went to Trinity College, and in 1829 won the university prize for a poem on *Timbuktu*.

In 1831 Tennyson's father died. Alfred's misery was increased by his Grandfather's discovery of his father's debts. He left Trinity College Cambridge, having entered in 1827, without taking a degree and his grandfather made financial arrangements for the family. The guiding hand for Alfred Tennyson came from his grandfather at Market Rasen.

In 1842 Alfred Tennyson published two volumes, which he certainly never excelled – never again equalled, thought his old Cambridge friend, Fitzgerald. Tennyson's success was secured; but as far as pecuniary profit went, it seems a mere *succeśs d'estime*. In 1845 Miles suggested to Sir Robert Peel that Tennyson should have a pension, and the state conferred on him £200 annually.

Alfred Tennyson

In 1850 Tennyson [see photo on left] was appointed poet laureate, in succession to Wordsworth, and soon after published *Ode on the Death of the Duke of Wellington.* In 1854 he composed *Maud,* a poem, which contains songs and lyrics of supreme beauty; and was the most profitable of his books up to this date. He bought some land at Farringford, in the Isle of Wight. Alfred Lord Tennyson passed away on October 6,1892.

When Bayons Manor was sold by Captain Alfred Tennyson d'Eyncourt, the estate was split up into lots, with farm and other tenants being given an initial option to purchase their holdings. Many of the houses in the village and much of the land passed into the hands of local buyers.

Mr. R.W. Drakes, who had farmed the manor and vale farms, acquired the bulk of the estate, including Bayons Manor and the parkland. Drakes later complained that vandals, who stripped lead off the Bayons Manor roof and ransacked it for souvenirs, made the mansion a very inconvenient possession.

In 1964 Drakes placed the still substantial estate on the market, and ironically, it was sold by auction by Mr. Geoffrey Cooper in the Corn Exchange, Market Rasen, the little market town, that the Tennysons had turned their backs on, during their rise to wealth and power, and deserted to build Bayons Manor. The buyer was Mr. Edward Sheardown of Castle Bytham, who paid £162,000 for the Bayons Manor estate, equivalent to £165 an acre. Included were the Manor Farm of 551 acres, the Vale Farm of 280 acres, Thorpe and Turnhill parks (135 acres) and the Deer Park (78 acres). Cottages and other buildings were also included. Mr. Sheardown announced after the sale, that Bayons Manor, the central feature of the estate would probably be demolished.

For Bayons Manor it was the last chapter. It had come full circle, and the fate of Bayons Manor was decided at Market Rasen. Seven months after purchase of the estate, Bayons Manor was blown sky high, towers and battlements and all, with enough dynamite to destroy a small town. As the dust cleared it could be seen that where once stood a picturesque piece of country scenery, lay a heap of rubble. The park, which had been laid out by Charles Tennyson-d'Eyncourt as a setting for a baronial castle, was ploughed up for cereal cropping.

The name of Tennyson now almost unknown in Market Rasen, which was where some were born, and the starting point for quite a remarkable family, who sadly, turned their backs on the little market town of Market Rasen.

The final chapter, in the chequered history of the Bayons Manor Estate at Tealby, came in 1972, when it was offered for sale by auction at Woodhall Spa. It was sold for approximately ¾ million pounds.

CHAPTER 28

THE 1960's TO THE 21st CENTURY

Looking up Queen Street

During the 1960's Market Rasen continued to offer a good service to the housewife, as the shopping habits continued to change. Lincoln was top of the shopping centres. In the ten-year period, 1961 to 1971, the Census of Distribution shows Lincoln sales had grown in real terms by 11.8 per cent. Gainsborough sales were up by 12.3 per cent. But Market Rasen sales increased over the ten years by an impressive 39.2 per cent, making it the third best performer among the smaller towns of Lincolnshire.

Brian Ward & Shirley Codd's Wedding

During this period, weddings were many in the town, one being [see photo] Mr Brian Ward [his parents greengrocers in Union Street] and Miss Shirley Codd [her brother Pete with me in the group on the Post Office steps]. The bridesmaid next to the bride is Jean Fell [her brother Des at the back]. Fell's had the Fish and Chip shop in Union Street, very clean, and the only ones who did scallops. Those were the days of top class fish and chips; however, I digress, back to the wedding. What a small world. While in the military I was on Special Security Duties RAFPD, I was told that a certain RAF Policeman, Count Coulson, who was on my Station [this a Special Atomic & Chemical Weapons Station and they came only on for shift from the Mother Station] was dating a young lady from Market Rasen whose parents had a fish and chip shop. It could only have been Jean Fell. I never did know the outcome. Another wedding, this to do with the Halpenny family, was in Canada in 1961 [see photo]. This was my cousin Pauline, my father's sister's daughter.

Wedding in the Halpenny family in Canada 1961

By the 1970's our eating habits were again changing, and so too, the shopping habits. Since 1960, the buses, considered as a major factor in connection with a shopping catchment plan, had fizzled out of contention. The village bus service, which replaced the carrier's cart, have they themselves followed them into history in many parts. Market Rasen has fewer buses in the 21st century. The shutters had gone up by now for many of the little shops in the side streets, and even those in the main street, were under threat. Empty shops were fast becoming a feature of the main street. People were in too much of a hurry, and housewives of the 1970's couldn't be bothered to ask what it is they want. Supermarkets were now the 'in-thing' for shopping, and people began to make shopping trips to Lincoln and other places. The service, civility, and the quality of goods, was a thing of the past. That may be so, but thankfully, the Spirit of the town was still burning bright at the senior citizens party [see photo] at the Working Men's Club, today [2004] called the Market Rasen Social Club.

Left to right – Ron New; Sheila Albone; Marion Cressey; Albert Rhodes; Harold Plumtree and Mrs Pat Clarke.

Sadly, the market town is full of estate agents, building societies and charity shops, all of which, kill a market town, and Market Rasen has paid the price. The opening picture [see photo] was taken on a wet Sunday afternoon in January 1986. Many people feared the competition from such giants as Woolworths and Marks and Spencers in the big towns, but these huge stores have found their place in the shopping pattern. This leaves the country town a real opportunity, to compete, for they can offer top quality fresh local produce, service and civility that is lacking in super stores. Market Rasen could be a boomtown, if only it would give the right local goods, quality and service, that a market town can offer. We are full circle for our needs, and with so much cheap imported rubbish, people want back the local natural produce, home produced pork pies and meats. What will kill that is genetically modified (GM) foods if not stopped now. In April 2004, 12 cows fed Syngenta's GM maize, died in very mysterious circumstances on a farm in the German state of Hesse. Naturally, there will be a cover-up, and the world will do nothing. That does ring a bell. A certain Bohemian Corporal, after attacking Poland, said: *"The world will hold its breath and do nothing."* They did and by then it was too late.

It was not only the shops that suffered. After a lapse of several years the Toc H movement started up again in Market Rasen in 1955. Toc H was a tiny seed that germinated in the Flanders Fields in1915. The organisation was founded at Poperinghe in Belgium, by the Rev. P.T.B. ('Tubby') Clayton just after the First World War. The aim of the movement was to uphold the ideals of fellowship and service. In 1922 it was incorporated by royal charter.

The clubhouse, which also served as a church, was named *Talbot House*, after a fallen officer. The army quickly reduced the name to initials, T.H., and lapsing into the signallers' habit of spelling out words spoken by telephone, came to know the place as 'Toc H', as we now say, Alpha Bravo Charlie, for ABC. Soon grew the expression *"He's as dim as a Toc H lamp."* The reason a Toc H lamp is dim, is that it is a traditional ancient oil lamp, and quite small. It is used in part of the ceremony at meetings. Sadly, with declining membership, coupled with the loss of its meeting rooms, the Market Rasen Toc H closed.

Of the 8 butchers in 1926, only one made it into the 21st century, that being Lancasters. Vin Lancaster took over and I remember him stood outside on a winter's day – gamebirds all hung out around the shop – swinging his arms into his body in order to keep warm. I also remember the day the black bullock got out into the street from the slaughterhouse. Vin's son Bill then took over the Family business [Thelma Lancaster, who was in my class at Mr Hancock's school, married John Bayes from the Gordon Arms] and today [2004] Bill's son Richard runs the Family business from their shops in the town.

Of the three Methodist chapels in Market Rasen, only one made it into the 21st century as a place of worship. From those early beginnings way back in the 1850's when the Primitive movement started with just six people, they flourished for a short time, only to fade away.

The breakaway Wesleyan Reformers started with the Victoria rooms as a temporary chapel. As their numbers increased they considered building a chapel of their own. This they did in 1852 and in 1859 they planned a new bigger chapel, and Mr. Chapman secured land in Union Street, upon which was built the Free Methodist Chapel. With changing times its doors were closed to worshippers, and sadly, this once proud house of God, was then used by Fossitt & Thorne, tyre company, and now even they have gone, just leaving a sad empty shell. The Jameson Bridge Street chapel is today [2003] used by the Freemasons. Like the Templars of old, the Freemasons have a Grand Master and carry out secret meetings.

Wesleyan Chapel

Only the Wesleyan Chapel survived as a place of worship. The building [see photo] is as imposing today as when it was first built.

The doctrines and practices of Pentecostalism came to Market Rasen, with the opening of the Pentecostal Hall in Oxford Street, just after the First World War. This Christian religious body never really got going in the Market Rasen area, and in the 1950's, children were the main congregation, mostly out of curiosity. The Pentecostal Hall was something out of the Wild West, just one room off the street. When a few of us lads went in early in the 1950's, the preacher then was Jimmie Jesus [right name as far as I know] and he wore Wellington boots. He was trying but it was uphill for him. Pentecostalism observes such practices as foot washing, diving healing, and spirit baptism, and that are generally fundamentalist in outlook. With no support, it was only a matter of time, and in the 1960's, the Pentecostal Hall closed its doors for the last time.

The train just made it into the 21st century, but it is running out of puff. The impressive station has been dismantled and the trains are getting as rare as rocking horse manure. No longer do trains pull in with horseboxes on race days, and the Station Master is no more.

Top left: On the left, just past the platform, stood the large Signal Box. Top right: A train enters the station on the down line. Above: The once proud and busy station now a sorry sight. A lone passenger waits ... High Noon.

In 1985, St. Thomas's Church at Market Rasen was again hit by vandals, and over £1000 worth of damage was done to south facing windows. The silver wafer box, which was stolen, has since been returned, but the brass tops from churchwarden's staves, which were also stolen, have not been found.

After continual structuring, Market Rasen is now bureaucratically controlled from Gainsborough, and it is difficult to see what benefits, if any, could flow from this distant form of centralisation, which ignored local interest and local ways of life.

There was more of a sense of purpose in many of the old vestry meetings of 100 years ago, than there is today, in many so-called town councils, whose purpose today is to give just a gentle nudge, on this or that subject, to the district council located at Gainsborough. The councils at local level have visibly been downgraded, and are nothing more than an anomalous part of the current 'Big Brother' structure. Market Rasen and the district around have demonstrably suffered in its democratic effectiveness.

The layout of the Caistor authority was derived from dispositions made at the time of the new Poor Law in 1834, while Rasen boundaries, quite extraordinarily, went back to the time of the monasteries, to the time when Middle Rasen Drax and Middle Rasen Tupholme were administered by different monasteries, leaving to Market Rasen at 976, a smaller actual acreage than any other authority anywhere in Lincolnshire. That was the noose around the town. But was it? That was not a problem with the right person at the helm; in fact, it could have been a blessing in disguise. I would have capitalised on it, and today you would have had a very rich and much sort after town that people would be proud of. It could have been the Mother of all market towns, not just in Lincolnshire, but also in the country. Those in power have no vision; more to the point, they are not interested, and Market Rasen suffered, and now in the 21st century pays the price for those idiots. You needed men or women [if not politically correct selected] who have vision, like Victor Lucas, who put Rasen racecourse on the world stage; or Mrs Smith who brought Rasen to town status; or Mrs Halpenny who put the right spirit, push for new business in the town, respect and made sure that those elected did their duty for the people and kept Rasen a town.

Throughout all the restructuring Market Rasen has paid the price. Caistor was restructured and re-built, and Rasen paid for that; Gainsborough was restructured and extended, and Rasen paid for that. Rasen remains forgotten, and for its council, paid the price, not for restructuring, but of neglect. There was nothing wrong with Market Rasen, just the town council and the county council. The area is good … the Roman's selected it, and the aerial view [see photo taken in 1970] shows the perfect place to settle. The large property is East House [you saw it in chapter 7 when thatched]. The trees in the grounds stretch from the copper beech [Doug Morley's] to the lime tree of Mr Bill Harris [my old De Aston School teacher]; Vin Booth's red tiled cottage is seen at rear of East house. Today [2003] little boxes built without thought, on every piece of land, in every back garden, even on land that floods. Waterloo Street will be flooded because of land built on Caistor Road. This is land I skated on in winter for flooded to depth of a few feet. No thought, and it can only bring BIG problems.

When rates were first levied at Market Rasen about 1890, the general district rate for the town brought in a sum of £1,196. The rate had been fixed at 3s. 6d in the pound, and Lindsey County Council sent a sum of £59- l0s -5d, to go towards the cost of repairing main roads running through the town. In 1985 the old class structure of the area has changed in a way which has produced an entirely different social back ground, with more managerial and administrative posts, being taken for granted, and because of this, Rasen was in many ways better-off in the days of the squires. As stated many times, the waywardness of the council bureaucracy leaves a lot to be desired, most should be on Gibbet's Corner.

To prove my point, in 2003, Market Rasen town councillor, Alf Jones, who has been at Rasen for some 40 years, said that the council have lost the 'plot' and should resign immediately. He also said that the equipment in the playing fields is pathetic; and, that he had never seen any accounts about the market place. They should not be kept secret.

Without any doubt, the best mayor that Market Rasen has ever had was old Tommie Bonnett. With his bowler hat upon his head, a cigarette in his mouth, he had a style and character of his own. His boundless enthusiasm was very comforting during the dark and uncertain days. Tommie Bonnett was chairman of the Urban Council throughout the 1914-18 war. No politically correct casting in those days. That is the problem today, too many 'yes men'; and no good will come until one gets rid of the politically correct do-gooders.

What then, is the great difference between our grandfathers day and our own? What have been lost are the marks of individuality that stand out a person of distinction. One Rasen character of distinction was Mrs. Caroline Fanny Smith, proprietor for a whole generation of Market Rasen's top ranking hostelry, the White Hart Hotel, which as you now know, is the sole reason why Rasen is a town.

Mrs. Smith was head of the Family and the Family business. She was the authority. On the one hand, she was a strict disciplinarian, but on the other hand, she was kind and thoughtful. Her customers were the best people of the district, and she mixed with them, not only as an equal, but also as one who was also familiar with still higher things. When she was a Lady in her teens, she had frequently visited her uncle, when he was engaged in constructing the railway, from Denmark to Germany, and on one occasion, she danced a quadrille with the then King of Denmark.

Nobody said whether she had the blood of some baron, count or duke running through her veins, but it could well have been so, for she had a film-star figure, gracious demeanour, and beauty that sparkled. At just turned 18 she married a gentleman farmer, who was destined [I think by way of agreement] to remain in the background. They had 10 children, but to see her, you would never have believed it, for she retained her film-star figure, demeanour and looks.

Of the personal relationship between Mr. and Mrs. Smith little is known. Rightly so, they kept their private life, private. Only one can be the captain, and it was Mrs Smith the one who gave the orders, from the sounding of the brass bell for the market ordinary luncheon on a Tuesday, to the proclaiming of a decision, which she regularly reached, that Mr So-and-so, sitting in one of the great Windsor chairs in her smoke room, should drink no more because it would not be good for him.

At this juncture, Mrs. Smith would personally intervene between customer and the barman, who was serving the drinks. Unceremoniously, and without a word, she would shut the serving window. There was no arguing, for all knew that her command was final. One might think that such action was high handed and likely to cause offence. But not with Mrs Smith in the White Hart Hotel, and perhaps also in a wider sphere, her authority was undeniable.

Mrs Smith was progressive, but at her pace and in her good time. At the White Hart Hotel she had gas installed in all her downstairs rooms, but did not do so for the upstairs rooms, thinking that the arrangements for candle lighting had been sufficient from the time before the Battle of Waterloo to the dawn of the 20th century; why, therefore, change such a romantic arrangement?

Mrs Smith was an astute business Lady. Her large four-wheeled carriage met every train arriving in Market Rasen station. She owned the only hearse in the town; as well as a great many horses and carriages, which were hired out. She had the best ostlers, and plenty of them.

She was a strict disciplinarian … one had to be in that period [just look now in the 21st century with being no deterrent] and her authority was unquestionable. It had to be. Nevertheless, she was kind and always ready to help those in need; be it soup for the poor, or medical needs for the sick.

Mrs Smith was a great Lady, and a Rasen character of distinction. She passed away peacefully at the age of 94, having run the White Hart Hotel from her bedroom, her coal fire all the time burning brightly, with the same precision and authority, as had marked her direction through the years that Rasen had been growing up.

The old White Hart building

Today, the White Hart is no more and where Mrs. Smith had her private room with canaries singing around her, it became first the office of Gordon Trill, the managing director of the Plastic Box Company; then the whole of the White Hart Hotel was turned into flats.

Why was it not preserved in its entirety?

If Mrs. Smith could only look down and see for herself, how the little market town that she made possible and helped to build, and the White Hart Hotel, which was then the centre of the town, [at the beginning, the Greyhound and the White Hart Hotel were in the centre, and faced the large open market place and the church. They then built on the west side of the market place, making it what it is today] had deteriorated, she would pull down the shutter and someone would be made to pay for the damage caused.

In her own lifetime, and against all the established customs of her age, she had stamped her personality, quite effortlessly, on her own town and her own setting, for without Mrs Smith giving the nod …plus a few free beers and a shilling or two … to the coachmen of the day, to change horses at Market Rasen, rather than Caneby Corner or at Middle Rasen, it is fact, that Market Rasen would never have become a town.

Another Rasen character of distinction was Mrs Eleanor May Halpenny, who in many ways was like Mrs Caroline Fanny Smith, but not with Family size, for Eleanor May had only 5 children; Joan, Derek, Gordon, John and Bruce Barrymore. Born into a Family of shopkeepers and landowners, Mrs Halpenny, like Mrs Smith, brought up on strict, but happy, conservative Christian, Family, Moral values. As you know, during the First World War, Eleanor May [Hall] went on munition work to help the war effort. During this period she met her husband to be, Harvey Ashton Halpenny, a Canadian soldier, who had been wounded at Vimy Ridge in France, and sent over to England for hospital treatment. With what little free time they had, Eleanor May and her work friends, would visit the wounded Servicemen in hospital, to bring them a little happiness, for many were a long way from home. On seeing the dashing Canadian soldier, it was love at first sight. They married in November 1917, and eventually Eleanor May took charge of the Family greengrocers business at 54 Queen Street, Market Rasen. Harvey settled in by doing the rounds to the country people, and he gave too many people credit, for many moved without paying.

During this period, Eleanor May had two bungalows built on the Willingham Road, and she controlled every brick laid. At that time the Family lived in a large wooden bungalow at the rear of the land, the back of which bordered Nettleship's orchard. The semi-detached bungalows were built at the front facing the Willingham Road; and even when moved into the new brick ones - Halpenny's lived in one bungalow, and her brother and his wife, Walter [see photo of uncle Walt, one seated] and Kath Hall, who had four sons, Dennis, Charlie (Chuck), Bill and Tony, lived in the other one - Eleanor May continued to use the large wooden one, which for the lads was great fun to sleep in. It was eventually sold to Jim Walsham [yes, the same Jim Walsham who had the 'Girl Friday' every day of the week], who took it down in sections and put it up on his property behind the petrol pumps on Willingham Road.

Walter Hall seated

Eleanor May then purchased No: 2 Willingham Road, Market Rasen, and this became the Halpenny Family home. At that period everything had to be in the man's name, even though purchased by Eleanor May. [Sadly this was sold whilst in Italy without my knowledge, but more about that in a moment] Mr and Mrs Halpenny moved in during the late 1920's. From 2, Willingham Road, Eleanor May ran 5 Clubs – Fattorini [first and only one in Lincolnshire], Empire Stores, Grattons, Freemans and Kays - Harvey worked for Perrelli, he organised the design and building of the electricity pylons that you see today across the country. He then worked as weigh man at the iron stone mine at Nettleton.

Like Mrs Smith, Mrs Halpenny was also a very astute business Lady, who was also ready to help people, and took no reward. She ran the Family home and Family business of five Clubs. Mrs Halpenny's Clubs flourished due to the fact that people trusted her; and, they were sold only top quality goods. The five Clubs were a shop window of top brand worldly goods, made available for a few pence a week; which Mrs Halpenny arranged and looked after. People got things they never dreamt possible. Because of this she built up a vast clientele, which included, rich and poor, young and old. The James, Boswells, Sorfleets, Pinkneys, Burkes, Coolings, Suttons, Allens, Fieldsends, Whites, Alisons, Toyntons, Brumptons, Campbells, Bayes, Wests, Chuck Smith, Fletchers, Lamiman, Maultbys, Bennets, Hancocks, Walkers, Codds, George, Ben, Henry Briggs, Blanchards, Barbara Jesnie and her mother; the list goes on and on. The people trusted Mrs Halpenny, and she never let them down.

As stated, 2 Willingham Road was open house to all Servicemen and women, so too to the Italian PoW's who were at Blakey's Mill. They were under the care of Mrs Halpenny.

No: 2 Willingham Road was a very happy Family home; and Christmas was always a delight. A very happy period. I have fond and happy memories of those Christmases. Never a cross word – just joyful times. There was always lovely coal fires burning brightly, and people were always welcome for a drink and mince pie. I remember Christmas 1944, for two coloured Americans were sent to Mrs Halpenny, but the house was full and they were sent away. When Eleanor May heard what someone had done, she sent me after them, and I brought them back for festive food and drinks. She had found room for two more – colour held no barriers at 2 Willingham Road.

During wartime rationing, Eleanor May purchased sweet coupons by the hundreds, but they were never used or sold. She bought them because people were desperate for money or traded for a bread loaf, and this was one way of helping. I remember seeing two large sweet jars full of coupons.

When she needed votes to get elected, Mrs Alda Nettleship, from the Manor House, would come to Mrs Halpenny, to ask her to make certain that all those in Long Twelve, Prospect Place, Willingham Road, Oxford Street and in other parts of the town, voted for her. The Taffy James of this world, did Mrs Halpenny's bidding for they trusted her, and she was always first to help them. Mrs Alda Nettleship, never once said "thank you" or ever went to thank the people in person. I know now, that she would never have got into power without the help of Mrs Eleanor May Halpenny; and, without the stern talk from Eleanor May, would never had made the stand to keep Rasen a town.

Mrs Halpenny never had a day in bed, she cooked all the meals, every day for all the Family, and she not only brought up her children [but also during the war years the evacuees], she also brought up Lance and Yvonne from Joan's [my sister] first marriage to Major Alf Boyce. They were brought up as part of the Family, and I was best man at Lance's wedding [see photo] at the back on left.

Lance Boyce's wedding

Mrs Smith and Mrs Halpenny were in many ways, two of a kind; Mrs Smith made Rasen a town … Mrs Halpenny kept Rasen a town. Like Mrs Smith, Mrs Halpenny also helped everyone. As stated, by having open house; buying coupons she did not need; paying in weekly money for people in order to keep their accounts in order; and then they paid her as and when they could; arranging votes for Mrs Alda Nettleship; and, she always loaned money when asked, but did not always get it back.

I remember Nick Hall, who was always welcome, was always at our house [see photo] taken in our back garden at Willingham Road. From the left: Bill Hall, Nick Hall, John Halpenny. Nick Hall came early every morning before going to

Bill, Nick and John

work, to sit in my place at the breakfast table, to write his bets for the horses, then leave his bets for Eleanor May to take to the bookies, but she was mostly too busy, and many times I took them round to Steve Godson. One morning, Nick Hall was crying when I came down stairs, for he had asked Eleanor May to loan him some money. She loaned him the money, more than once. Many times Nick Hall has passed me in the street and has never spoken. What a short memory, but I haven't.

Mrs Halpenny paid the deposit on property for many people, one being for Sue [her sister] Egan's property in Oxford Street. She never got any thanks, and in some cases, never got the full money back. Society and families were certainly changing, but not for the better. It is a long lane that has no turning.

Derek Halpenny's wedding to his second wife

Market Rasen never had a main family in control, and it is easy to see why. Take the Halpenny Family, well placed, large Family, plenty of contacts, but jealously was always simmering, but never when with Hannalore [Derek's first wife]. I was best man at Derek's wedding to his second wife [see wedding photo] and now he does not speak. Guilty conscience I expect. Whilst in Italy, and knew of nothing that was going on, my father passed away, and Derek sold up the Family home without giving me a chance to purchase it. It was sold to Peter Rhodes who I contacted and offered him double what he paid, to get it back, but he would not sell. Derek had no right to sell the Family home for Mrs Halpenny was still alive, but Derek was the sole executor and all left to his two children, and had to be sold. But sold so quickly, before I could get back from Italy. How strange, that only Derek's two children should inherit all the Family home and it had to be sold up, with him being the only executive.

At 2 Willingham Road were all my childhood memories, my annuals and toys, which included 700 lead soldiers. They had all gone. I was not offered anything from the Family home, not even my toys and books (which were my property); and, contrary to what many people think, I did not get one penny piece from the sale of our property, nor did I get any of my childhood toys, books and annuals Rupert, Film Fun, Knockout, Beano, Dandy [now worth a lot of money]. I got only the picture of my father and this I had to go and ask for. It was handed to me on the doorstep. I went with Yvonne to get it and two pictures, which Lance wanted, and these are all we got. When Derek brought them out, I asked him why the Family home was sold when mother was still alive. It was her property. She bought it. He snapped: *"As far as I'm concerned, I do not have a mother."* When asked about all my things that were my property, and my father's pocket watch, which he had given to me and was left at the Family home, the door was slammed shut in my face. That could never have been so if Hannalore had still been alive. Hannalore, his first wife, would not have stood for this evil act, that is a fact, but she was now no longer around, and her warm loving nature sadly died with her, to be replaced by Derek's hate, jealousy and greed.

Derek Halpenny deeply hurt his own mother when he passed her in Tesco's, it is hard to imagine that he just gave a cold, angry stare, and did not speak. This to his own mother who had not done a thing wrong to him, and done so much for him. To think this man then became a justice of the peace. No wonder no justice. That hurt

Eleanor May deeply, and she came to me crying. She started Derek with a £1,000 when he came out of the Forces with Hannalore, his very beautiful bride, who knew only love and kindness and thought the world of Eleanor May. Just before he was demobbed, Eleanor May purchased for Derek a front room full of coffee beans, for him to take back to Germany, for coffee beans were more important than either the English pound or the American dollar. The coffee bean was king and could buy anything.

What little market towns like Market Rasen owe to the driving force and personalities of people like Mrs Caroline Fanny Smith and Mrs Eleanor May Halpenny, we shall never know.

Now in a politically correct age, which is completely corporate in its practice and corrupt, people think whimsically of such personalities as Mrs Smith and Mrs Halpenny, because they are so distant from them, not only in years but also in spirit.

But examples like these, which stand out in Rasen history, remind us that many things never change, and in the 21st century, with the breakdown of trust between neighbours, and with no such people like Mrs Smith and Mrs Halpenny to hold the social fabric of the people and town together, things can only go from bad to worse.

In a period of swift technological and social change it is a great pity that Market Rasen has lost so many of its shops and services. With the decline the number of estates in the area fell away very markedly. Market Rasen council should have seen it coming and expanded. The thinking was, that the little towns such as Market Rasen depend on the farming villages, which they serve, and without support from their villages, the market towns are deprived of a main part of their function … Bunkum! There has to be winners and losers. If Market Rasen offered the right climate, the right facilities, the right services, and the right products, people would use the town, not because they had to, but because they wanted to.

Market Rasen was once the 'Real Countryside' but not now. It needs people with drive and vision, who thinks and does for the town; and, most of all, Common Sense, not politically correct do-gooders by the likes of the Nazi Co-op. We fought two world wars to remove this NAZI teaching; now, you are letting it flood back. By kind permission of the Countryside Alliance, I publish unabridged, Mr Stanton's letter on co-op chickens that appeared in their spring 2003 edition of their magazine. Not only do they poison your mind, but at £5-75 a pound they rook you in the bargain. Here is, the unbelievable … unbelievable that you good citizens should let it happen.

Real Countryside SPRING 2003 59

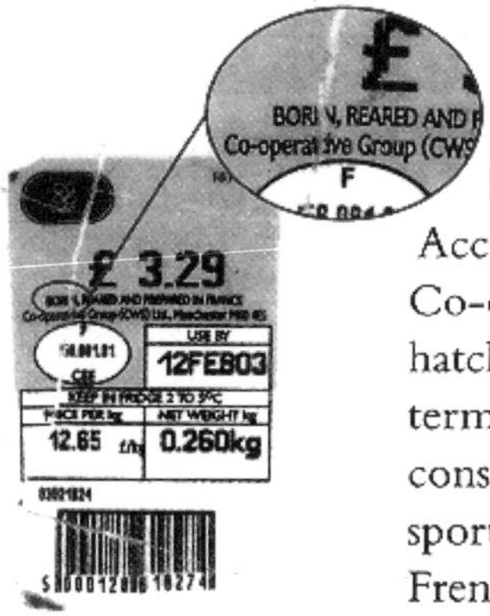

WINNING LETTER:
BORN FREE

According to the label (shown left) from the Co-op, chicks are now 'born', and not hatched. This ludicrously sentimentalised terminology misleads children, and is entirely consistent with the Co-op's stance on rural sports. Incidentally, this French (why French?) chicken works out at £5.75 per lb.

M Stanton, Watlington, Oxon

To the passing eye, Market Rasen has everything such a place should have. But stop for a moment. It only has some good inns and taverns, without them, it has sod all. Market Day is almost a thing of the past. During the 1950's and the 1960's, the little market town, after two world wars, was back in business; the market was filled with poultry (live and dead) rabbits by the dozen (live and dead), pheasants and other game, and all the garden and farm produce you could imagine. Market stalls of every kind filled the market place to over flowing, and when the auctions were over the farmers were doing deals in the Gordon Arms, Aston Arms, George, and the Greyhound.

Wednesday is cattle market day, held on the Linwood Road, and in 1985 still owned, as was the market place until recently, by the Nettleship family, and with the passing of Mrs. Alda Nettleship, her son Nicholas, who never went to any school in Rasen [obviously not good enough] and does not live in the town, owns and controls it like a lot of other property in the town. Only a trickle of livestock now passes through the market.

It was the stagecoaches, which met at Market Rasen … thanks due to Mrs Smith that made the place a thriving market town. The coaches came and went and the railway reached Market Rasen, but only a few trains stop today ...well maybe. It is almost a ghost station as it crumbles into history. The market has gone. The purpose built post office from the main street has gone. The spirit of the market town has gone. The buses have followed the carrier's cart into history, with only a new bus service put in place in 2004, and that is a route from Lincoln to Cleethorpes, passing through Market Rasen. But then most people on their way to the coast speed quickly through Market Rasen for the little market town has only memories to offer. As we enter the 21st century, Market Rasen is fighting to stay on the map, and remain an English market town. It could do so with ease, if it got back that old wartime spirit and the right people.

On the left is the liberal club – now part of the doctors' bigger surgery [opened 1991], which is the new building adjacent to it. The surgery is built on the site of the old gasometer. On the right is a car park and in the background is the library.

But, sadly, the sands of time are running out for Market Rasen to remain an English Market Town. Already, pushed along by the politically correct, do-gooders, pervert judges, the waywardness of the councils, Market Rasen's culture, heritage and traditions, such as coursing [fishing will be next] and the traditional Family Christmas and Christmas Tree, have gone. Gone also Common Sense and innocent child-hood games and pastimes such as conkers, marbles, sledging, rocking horses, toy six-shooters and holsters for playing Cowboys and Indians [talking of Indians will explain about Pocahontas in a moment], and comics that I had as a young lad, are either banned as dangerous or not politically correct.

Rasen market day in the 21st Century ... the cars speed quickly through.

The legendary Billy Bunter of Greyfriars School, in 1992 was barred from the BBC for being … wait for it …stoutest, racist and not the slightest politically correct. The bespectacled Bunter, consumer of cream buns and pop [like any normal lad], first appeared in the Magnet Comic in 1908, and brought pleasure to millions, myself included, for Billy Bunter was in the Knockout Comic that I had on a Wednesday. Enid Blyton books have made normal children happy for well over 50 years, now they have been re-written for too sexist and racist. Out has gone Noddy's golliwog friend, and there are now no references to Toy town folk looking gay or Noddy 'feeling queer'. Might upset judges and members of parliament I expect. Then they should not read Noddy if it upsets them. This means a nation of politically correct cissies, not normal healthy men and women. I remember the Nazi's burning books in the streets, because these books were not politically correct. Political Correctness is nothing more than dictatorship.

England is not the country that all those beneath the apple-crate crosses in Europe and other foreign fields, fought for. What they fought and gave their lives for has gone – swamped by vast numbers of so-called asylum seekers, who demand their language and culture, and do not integrate – like the Italians, Germans, Poles and others did during and after the Second World War. They soon learned English and there were no problems. Now let me give you another example … Pocahontas [c.1595-1617], daughter of the mighty American Red Indian Chief Powhatan in Virginia, who, when 12 years old, saved the life of Captain John Smith, a son of Lincolnshire, and one of the Jamestown colony leaders, who had been captured by the Indians. Held by the English as a hostage, she married a Captain Rolfe [1614], and in 1616 went with her husband to England, and sadly, died at Gravesend of smallpox. A statue and two memorial windows in the city church of St Sepulchre commemorate Princess Pocahontas. Pocahontas integrated without any problems and she bore her husband a son. Pocahontas learned the English language, which she spoke fluently, converted to Christianity, and took the name Rebecca. She was laid to rest in St George's churchyard in Gravesend, Kent. The beautiful princess won the love of the English people, and she was made most welcome; indeed, Queen Anne graciously received her. I mention Pocahontas, for she integrated and brought only love and kindness to England. She obviously did heed the advice to St Augustine: *'When in Rome, live as the Romans do; when elsewhere, live as they live elsewhere'*. Not to do so, can only lead to Big Problems. The writing was on the wall in 2003, when Scotland Yard said that they had thwarted more than 30 gangland murders involving the same crime gangs among immigrant communities.

Times change, that is a fact; but they do not always change for the better. Take the 21st century clubs. Today [2004] you have very little choice and it is a fact that you are not a valued customer. It is also a fact that Eleanor May Halpenny would not have accepted the 21st century club con, and would have done as I have done here …EXPOSED IT. When you good people, telephone in good faith, telephone numbers that start with either 0870 or 0871 [they now try to mask this scam by showing five digits, but it is the first four that count] companies – that includes all the big ones like Argos, Chums, Deanes [part of Chums], J.D. Williams, Oxendales, Heather Valley, to name but a few – can be earning 3 pence or more a minute from your call. Now you will understand why you are kept on hold, and kept being told very busy and that your call is important. They are playing you for a Sucker. Eleanor May never sold any bad goods and would have sent them packing, for her customers were first and foremost and would not have stood for that cheap underhand scam. So, trade where you see an honest number and shun all those greedy non-geographic 0870, 0871 and 090x numbers, and save yourself a lot of time and money.

For Market Rasen to remain an English Market Town, it will need strong, honest leadership from the Rasen people, who, like Mrs Caroline Fanny Smith and Mrs Eleanor May Halpenny, thought and worked for Market Rasen and its people. They built and kept it an English Market Town … now the people of Rasen must unite as one, and let Common Sense prevail, if they wish to remain a normal, sane, healthy in mind and body, happy and safe … English Market Town.

The End?